BETH MEAD

TO MUM, I KNOW YOU WOULD LOVE THIS BOOK

With thanks to Matt Oldfield

First published in Great Britain in 2023 by Wren & Rook

ISBN: 978 1 5263 6586 6
Exclusive Signed Edition ISBN: 978 1 5263 6629 0

1 3 5 7 9 10 8 6 4 2

MIX
Paper from
responsible sources
FSC www.fsc.org FSC® C104740

Wren & Rook
An imprint of
Hachette Children's Group
Part of Hodder & Stoughton
Carmelite House
50 Victoria Embankment
London EC4Y 0DZ

An Hachette UK Company
www.hachette.co.uk
www.hachettechildrens.co.uk

Printed and bound in Great Britain by Clays Ltd, Elcograf S.p.A.

BETH MEAD

Illustrated by Mark Long

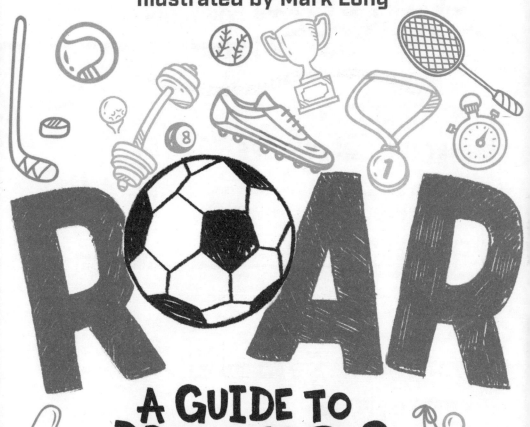

ROAR

A GUIDE TO DREAMING BIG AND PLAYING THE SPORT YOU LOVE

wren
&rook

CONTENTS

INTRODUCTION

Hi there! My name is Beth Mead – welcome to my book, welcome to my world.

In July 2022, my life changed completely when the Lionesses went all the way and **won the UEFA Women's Euro trophy**. Remember that? Maybe you saw the final on TV, or maybe you were one of the lucky eighty-seven thousand fans who got to watch it live at Wembley Stadium. Well, I'm very proud to say that I was part of that amazing winning team. In fact, I won the **Best Player** and **Top Scorer of the Tournament awards** for my six goals and five assists.

But that success is only one part of my story. What I want to do in this book is share the **whole journey**: from the girl growing up in North Yorkshire to the professional footballer playing for Arsenal and England. Why? **Because I want to inspire YOU to find YOUR sporting passion and follow YOUR dreams**, just like I did.

For me, sport is a very special thing and it's about so much more than just playing a game. It's about fun, freedom, friendship, focus and flair, and those are just the words beginning with 'f'!

Please trust me when I say this:

SPORT HAS THE
MAGIC POWER
TO CHANGE YOUR LIFE.

As you're about to find out, I have football to thank for many of the greatest moments of my life, as well as many of my best friends, and it's helped me achieve great things both on and off the pitch. In fact, the skills you learn from sport **can help you accomplish anything you put your mind to**.

The path to the top is never straightforward. Along the way, there are ups and downs, high and lows, but step by step, chapter by chapter, I'll be there by your side, sharing the messages that I wish I could have given myself when I was young like you. Important messages like:

and

and

Because if you're doing something you love, with passion and joy, there's nothing you can't achieve.

Sounds exciting, right? But before we head off on this incredible sporting journey together, we should probably get to know each other a bit better. So I'm going to ask you **three questions** that I had to answer once, during a football team-building trip, as we sat around a campfire eating marshmallows:

1) What's your favourite number and why?

2) What scares you the most?

3) What's the weirdest thing you've ever had to eat or drink?

Killer questions, eh? I'll tell you my answers first and give you some extra time to think:

0:12

1) Sorry, I'm going to cheat and pick two: seven and nine. And why? **Football, of course!** Seven because I loved **David Beckham** as a kid and so wore that number on the back of my shirt. Nine because that was the number I've worn for most of my professional career, and also my birthday is on the ninth.

2) Easy: spiders! I just don't understand why they have eight legs. **Why does anything need eight legs?!**

3) At England camps when I was younger, we used to have these little beetroot energy drinks. They're supposed to be really good for you and give you a boost, but **URGH**, they tasted like soil to me!

So there you go: some fun facts about me. Now it's your turn! If you're still struggling to think, try eating a few marshmallows. That's my first bit of advice in this book - marshmallows make anything easier!

OK, time to get this adventure started – are you ready to

ROOOAAARRR?

BETH'S PRE-CHAPTER WARM-UP: THE HOPSCOTCH

Here's the hopscotch warm-up to wake up those sleepy feet and get you moving. It's good for:

- ✓ Co-ordination
- ✓ Concentration
- ✓ Speed
- ✓ Agility

WHAT TO DO: Using chalk, mark out a ten-square hopscotch grid on the ground outside.

YOUR CHALLENGE: Hop from square to square, first going up to ten, and then turning back round and hopping back to one. Try to complete the grid without missing any squares and time yourself over five sets to see if you can get quicker each time!

EXTRA TIME: Too easy? Do it backwards!

TWIST IT UP: Draw a hopscotch grid on a piece of paper and get someone to call out numbers one to ten in a random order. When you hear a number, you've got to tap it with your hand. See how fast you can do it!

CHAPTER ONE

JUMP IN AND ENJOY!

Right, I want to kick things off with a simple but very important question:

WHO LOVES SPORT?

Now, seeing as you're reading my book (thanks, by the way!), your answer may well be, **'YES, ME!'** If that's you waving your arm high in the air, then brilliant. But some of you may be sat shaking your heads. Maybe you're reading this book because you enjoyed watching the Lionesses go all the way at Euro 2022, but when it comes to playing sport yourself, you think it's not for you. Well, let me stop you right there, because . . .

SPORT IS FOR EVERYONE!

OK, so you're probably not going to love every single one you try, but if you jump in and give lots of them a go, eventually I'm sure you'll find at least one sport that you really enjoy. It certainly worked that way for me.

As a kid growing up in a little village in North Yorkshire, I was a free spirit with **A LOT of energy**. (If you've ever seen me play football for England or Arsenal, you probably won't be surprised to hear that!) By the time I turned five, my parents were already looking for a way to tire out their very active daughter, so which sport did they sign me up for – **football? Cricket? Hockey?** No, instead my mum took me to a class at the local village hall:

BALLET!

REALLY, MUM?!

SPOILER ALERT: it turned out that ballet wasn't for me. I hated the leotard, the tutu and the shoes, and, personally, I found the classes slow and boring. I had way **too much energy** to hold the positions for long, and all that time standing still gave cheeky little me lots of chances to cause mischief. The teacher often had to lead me outside by the wrist and over to my mum, to tell her that I was disrupting the others. **Sorry, Frances!**

Mum didn't give up, though. She wanted me to do at least one ballet exam, so she came up with an offer that she knew **I couldn't refuse**. If I passed, we would finally get the family pet that we'd been talking about for ages, the pet that I'd always wanted: **A DOG**! With my very own puppy for motivation and up for grabs, I worked hard enough to pass that first exam, and we got Jess, our beautiful Border Collie. But sadly for Mum, that was more than enough ballet for me and my career soon came to an end.

By the way, **I THINK BALLET IS BRILLIANT**. You can improve your posture, health and even your co-ordination by doing it, and it takes a lot of stamina to hold those amazing poses. **But it just wasn't the right activity for ME.**

OK, so then what was? It was time to try other sports that might suit me better. What I wanted to do was run around with a purpose, having fun and feeling free. Now, what sport would let me do that?

It's time to get thinking:

What kind of activity do YOU want to do? Something where it's just you against an opponent? Something where you're part of a team? Something where you have set routines to learn? Something where you do the same activity again and again? Something where anything can happen?

And how do YOU want to feel? **FREE? CALM? FOCUSED? DETERMINED? HAPPY? EXCITED?**

A year later, when I was six, Mum took me down to the local village sports field one Saturday morning to try a different activity:

FOOTBALL!

NICE ONE, MUM – MUCH BETTER!

14

My family have **always loved football**, and my dad and uncle both played in a local Sunday league. With their help and encouragement, I had already mastered the basic skills of controlling the ball and kicking with both feet. But so far, all I knew was kickarounds at home or in the park with the local kids and crab football in PE class (you know, the game where you scuttle around with your hands and feet on the floor, kicking a ball? **It's so much fun!**). Now I was about to play the game properly.

When I walked out on to the pitch, the coach welcomed me warmly, but he was quick to warn my mum: **'Most of the players are boys and they can be a bit . . . rough. Will she be OK?'**

'She'll be fine,' Mum replied straight away. 'She's got lots of energy and she loves running around.' Plus, she knew that I wouldn't mind **a bit of rough play at all**!

Was I nervous? Maybe a little bit, but mainly **I was excited**. I knew most of the boys already from the village, and I had played enough football to know that a) it suited me, and b) I liked it **A LOT** better than ballet! So when the session started, I jumped right in. I wanted to be involved in everything: taking every throw-in, every corner, every free-kick . . . and I enjoyed every minute of it. By the end, I had played every position on the pitch and proved a few people wrong.

'WOW, SHE'S VERY GOOD,'

THE COACH TOLD MY MUM,

'AND SHE'S ROUGHER THAN MOST OF THE BOYS!'

Thanks, coach! From that day forward, I was totally hooked on football, but I didn't just stop there. I kept jumping in and trying new things because **I really did love all sports**, and I was good at them too. At primary school, PE was my favourite lesson, and break and lunch time were my favourite parts of the day. I signed up for every after-school club and every event at Sports Day: the sack race, the running race, the egg and spoon race . . . and **I always made sure that I finished first**! Later on at secondary school, I got to try even more sports, like **netball, hockey and athletics. I COULDN'T GET ENOUGH OF THEM.**

I was playing lots of sports outside of school too, including some that I hadn't even signed up for. I

remember one morning after football training, I went along to watch my younger brother, Ben, running in a cross country race. When we arrived, one of the girls hadn't turned up, so they asked me to take her place. **Really, did I have to?** I'd just played football! Eventually, I did say yes, though, and I was so competitive that I ended up winning the race and qualifying for the next round!

Our village also had a junior boys' cricket team, and I often played for them during the summers, along with my brother. Ben was never the best footballer (unfortunately for him, I think I got that gene!), but he was a good cricketer. I wasn't bad either, but I was a bit too impatient for batting; I just wanted to **whack the ball as far as possible every time**! Instead, with my concentration and hand-to-eye co-ordination, I was best at fielding. That's one of the things I love best about sport: you can't be good at every single part, but that's OK. If you acknowledge the bits you can do well, you can play to your strengths and win as a team. In one amazing match, I took two catches while Ben was bowling. The story even made the local newspaper, with the headline:

'THE MEAD SHOW'!

I enjoyed pretty much all of the different sports I played, but usually there was at least one thing that stopped me from falling in love:

HOCKEY – I didn't want to wear a skirt while playing sport

CROSS COUNTRY – I wanted to do more than just run

SWIMMING – I wanted to do more than just swim (from one end of the pool to the other)

CRICKET – I wanted the action to be faster

For me, there was just **one sport that was only positives** and no negatives, that always stayed at the very top of my list: **FOOTBALL**.

Why? It's hard to explain, but I just loved the feeling of freedom as I raced around the pitch, chasing and kicking the ball with no worries or other thoughts in my head. **Oh, and the rush of scoring goals, of course!** Yes, football was definitely the sport for me, no doubt about it. No other game gave me that same level of enjoyment and excitement, and it still makes me feel the same way now, twenty amazing years later.

But enough about me for this chapter, because this book is also about YOU and YOUR favourite things to do.

Don't worry, I'm not expecting you to love **ALL sports** like me. One of my best friends, Alex, wasn't very interested in playing sport and when I was younger, I always found that difficult to understand. Why didn't she want to chase a ball around a field, scoring goal after goal, like me? As I've got older, though, I've come to realise that we're all different and we all like different things. **What a boring place the world would be if we all shared exactly the same passions?!** Alex has always been a really caring person, and she now works in a nursing home, looking after people and helping to make them happy. What an amazing job that is!

So whether you already love sports like me or you're just tip-toeing your way on to the start line of your sporting journey, **EVERYONE IS WELCOME HERE**.

There are lots of different accessible and disability sports, like Goalball, for example. Goalball is a three-a-side indoor sport for people who are blind or partially sighted. The ball has bells inside it that make noise, so the players can track it as it moves. The aim of the game is to score goals by bowling the ball along the floor, and into the other team's net.

SOUNDS AWESOME!

Many sports can also be adapted so that if you have a disability, you can still play the sport you love. For example, there's wheelchair tennis, inclusive dance, deaf basketball, sitting volleyball, autism-friendly trampoline sessions where the music is turned down, plus loads more. You can also join disabled-only or mixed teams, depending on your preference. **For more information on different organisations that offer accessible and inclusive activities, check out the resources page at the end of this book.** And if you need some more ideas, just have a look at incredible Paralympians like swimmer **Ellie Simmonds**, wheelchair racer **Hannah Cockroft** and cyclist **Sarah Storey**, or watch the Great Britain national wheelchair rugby team win the Gold medal at Tokyo 2020.

WHAT AMAZING ATHLETES!

OK, READY TO GET TO WORK?

GET READY TO ROAR ACTIVITY

1. On a piece of paper, I want you to write down a list of your Top 3 sports, starting with your favourite at number one. If you can, add in the reason why you **LOVE** each one so much!

2. Then, below, make a second list, this time with the Top 3 new sports that you'd **like to try and why**. Does your school offer any of these activities already? If not, could you ask a teacher or family member about how to get started?

If you're struggling to write any down, have a think about the sports you like watching. Perhaps there is a sport on the telly that looks fun, or beautiful or just really entertaining. Is this something you could try?

Still can't think of anything? Try the flow chart on the next page to help you choose.

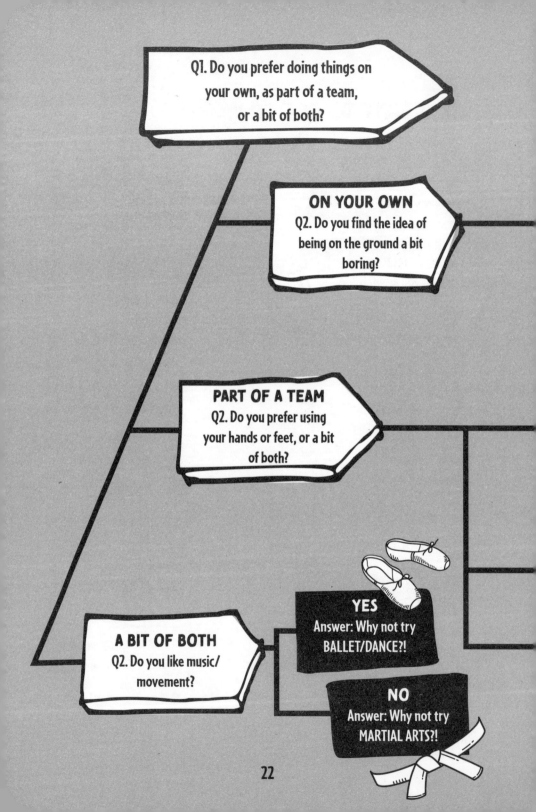

Q1. Do you prefer doing things on your own, as part of a team, or a bit of both?

ON YOUR OWN
Q2. Do you find the idea of being on the ground a bit boring?

PART OF A TEAM
Q2. Do you prefer using your hands or feet, or a bit of both?

A BIT OF BOTH
Q2. Do you like music/ movement?

YES
Answer: Why not try BALLET/DANCE?!

NO
Answer: Why not try MARTIAL ARTS?!

22

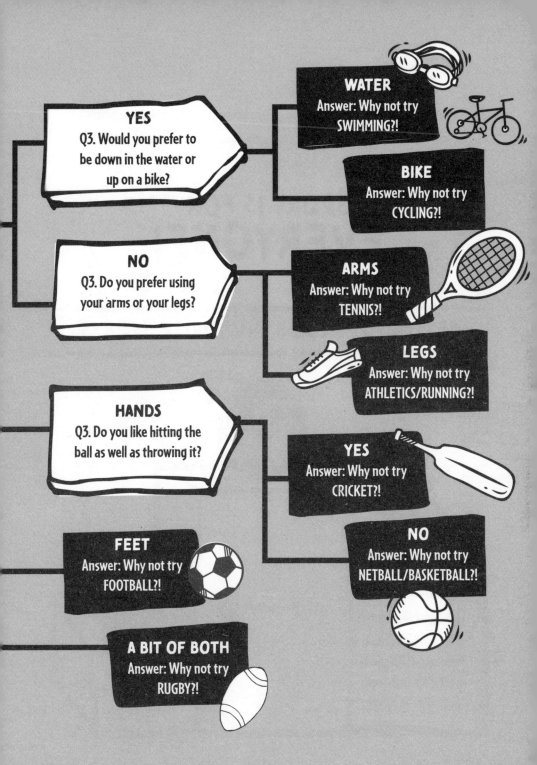

YES
Q3. Would you prefer to be down in the water or up on a bike?

WATER
Answer: Why not try SWIMMING?!

BIKE
Answer: Why not try CYCLING?!

NO
Q3. Do you prefer using your arms or your legs?

ARMS
Answer: Why not try TENNIS?!

LEGS
Answer: Why not try ATHLETICS/RUNNING?!

HANDS
Q3. Do you like hitting the ball as well as throwing it?

YES
Answer: Why not try CRICKET?!

NO
Answer: Why not try NETBALL/BASKETBALL?!

FEET
Answer: Why not try FOOTBALL?!

A BIT OF BOTH
Answer: Why not try RUGBY?!

I know trying new things can be scary sometimes, especially if you think that thing isn't for you. But remember what I said back at the start of this chapter:

SPORT IS FOR
EVERYONE!

BETH'S TOP THREE FAVOURITE SPORTS:

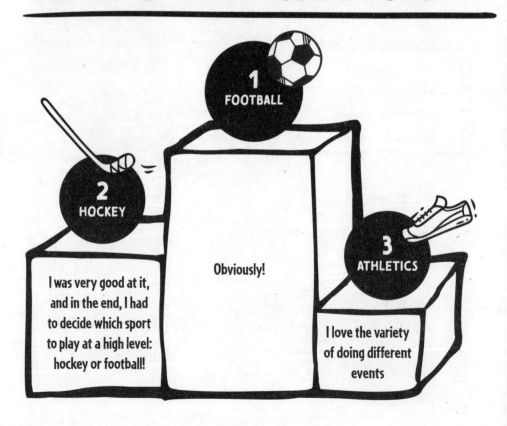

1 FOOTBALL

Obviously!

2 HOCKEY

I was very good at it, and in the end, I had to decide which sport to play at a high level: hockey or football!

3 ATHLETICS

I love the variety of doing different events

Hero: Dame Kelly Holmes

One of my favourite sporting events to watch has always been the Olympics. It just has this different feel to a football tournament, for example. There's something so special about the best athletes from all over the world, and from lots of different sports, coming together to compete against each other. I love watching it all on TV, whatever sport is on.

One of my first and favourite Olympic memories was watching **Kelly Holmes** win two gold medals at the 2004 games in Athens, in the 800m and 1500m races. At the time, I was a nine-year-old girl who was quite good at running, so to watch a British woman cross that finish line in first place and become a **double world champion** was so exciting and inspiring. **I can still picture her winning smile now!**

I was lucky enough to meet Kelly many years later, after the Lionesses won the Euros. We had a really nice chat, and soon afterwards, I followed in her footsteps by winning the BBC Sports Personality of the Year award. **The nine-year-old me would not believe it!**

BETH'S PRE-CHAPTER WARM-UP: WOW WORDS

Are you ready to roar? Sometimes getting noisy can help you to feel more energised, just like when we hear the fans as we run out into the stadium – it gives us a huge lift and makes us want to do our best. It's good for:

- ✓ Making you happy
- ✓ Boosting confidence
- ✓ Releasing nerves
- ✓ Energising you

WHAT TO DO: Think of some wow words that someone said to you recently. It could be something like: **you're the best goal scorer; you're a brilliant friend; you make me happy!**

YOUR CHALLENGE: Look at yourself in the mirror and say those wow words to yourself with a big smile. Do it five times – get louder each time.

EXTRA TIME: Make a poster with your wow words and stick it on your wall – say those words every morning before school!

CHAPTER TWO

BE HAPPY IN WHO YOU ARE AND CREATE YOUR OWN KIND OF FUN

So, do you feel like you've already found **YOUR** favourite sport?

If you have, that's great – we'll look at ways you can raise your game and find your **superstar switch** later in this book, to help you become a star player! But don't worry if you haven't just yet. As I said before, and I'll keep saying throughout this book, **we're all different**. For some people like me, that passion for a particular sport might arrive straight away after one super-fun session. For some, it will grow gradually over time, and for others, it could take years of trying lots of different things.

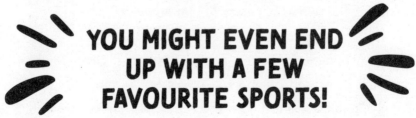

YOU MIGHT EVEN END UP WITH A FEW FAVOURITE SPORTS!

But whichever way, that's OK. Because the most important thing is having fun playing sport and doing what **YOU** want to do.

I know it's not always easy to follow your own path in life, especially when you might feel a pressure to fit in. But it's so important to always be yourself and

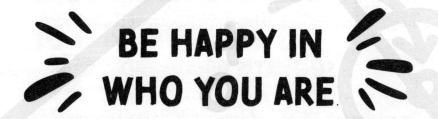

BE HAPPY IN WHO YOU ARE.

Growing up, I didn't always want to do the same things that my friends did, but I never let that stop me, and neither should you. Whatever it is that you love doing, **do it with passion and without fear of other people judging you**.

In Hinderwell, the village where I grew up, I was surrounded by sea, fields, moors and beaches. It's a beautiful place to live, but for a young kid with energy to burn, there really wasn't a lot going on. So we had to create fun for ourselves.

On bright summer days, the local kids would all go down 'The Back Lane', a path behind my gran's house that led out of the village and into the corn fields beyond. There, we would jump around on hay bales and do other silly stuff like that, until someone came and told us off.

But the rest of the time, the boys were busy doing what they loved best: playing football for hours and hours. The other girls preferred to just sit on the swings in the park, chilling and chatting. It was nice, but I'd get bored easily. I was way too energetic and active, and **I wanted to be out there playing football**.

SO THAT'S WHAT I DID.

The small playing field next to the park only had one goalpost, which never had a net in it. But if there were enough kids around for a proper match, we'd put down jumpers for goalposts at the other end to make a full pitch. I loved those competitive games, yet there was one big problem: without a net, every time you'd shoot and score, you'd have to chase after the ball, and often jump over a fence to get it back!

After a while, that got pretty annoying. So we came up with a better idea. There was an industrial estate nearby

and we asked the owners if we could use the garage doors for our football practice. Fortunately, they said yes and they even let us spray-paint on a crossbar. **HURRAY!** Our new pitch was perfect, especially for games of headers and volleys. Now, whenever I scored a great goal, the ball bounced straight back to me – **MUCH BETTER**!

Ah, those were the days: freedom and endless football. The local boys never treated me any differently because I was a girl. I liked to play, and I was good at it, so I was part of the gang. It was as simple as that. **I wasn't thinking about the differences between us**; I was just doing what I wanted to do, what made **ME** happy.

But I know that not everyone is lucky enough to have such a positive experience. Sometimes groups of kids can be cliquey and hard to break into. If you're trying to play football with a group who won't let you join their game, be patient and try watching from the sidelines for a bit. Hopefully, you'll get your chance to shine eventually, and if not? Well, there are plenty of other games to play. And if you're in a team and someone wants to join, **let them in**! They might be an awesome player and help make your team even better.

OK, back to me and my days of endless football. If I wasn't out in the village or the school playground playing, I was back home practising with my dad or making my brother stand in the doorway of our hall so I could kick balls past him – or at him. Either or. I used to love bossing him around. **Well, until he got bigger than me . . .**

So yes, growing up, playing football with boys was just the norm for me. It was all I knew, and I loved it. But what about playing with girls? Well, that came a bit later, and at first, I hated it. Phil, my first football coach, could see that I had a lot of talent, and he suggested that I should find a girls team to play for. The nearest one, Middlesbrough, was an hour's drive away from Hinderwell, so a couple of nights a week, Dad would take me up there to indoor training sessions, **and every time, I would cry and run out**.

Because it was a **scary new environment** for me, where everyone else knew each other, and I knew no one. I didn't feel like I fitted in. The other girls were all from Middlesbrough, a town, whereas I was a country girl.

SUDDENLY, I WAS A LITTLE FISH IN A BIG, UNFAMILIAR POND.

Have you ever felt like you didn't fit in? If so, what did you do about it?

I hope you didn't let it stop you from doing what you wanted to do. **Keep going; follow your path!** If you do feel like you don't fit in, my advice would be to talk to someone you trust about it: *a friend, a teammate, a coach, a family member.* It's always good to speak up and share these things because the truth is, **most of us at some point in our lives will feel this way and you're not alone**.

You can also play a part in helping others to feel welcome too. For example, if you have someone new at your school, or at sports practice, go and say hello. Introduce yourself and ask them what their interests are. **I'll bet you'll find something in common and they'll feel happy in your team.**

Fortunately, with my parents behind me, I kept going with football. During those miserable early sessions at Middlesbrough, there was a scout watching me from a team called 'California'. No, sadly it was nothing to do with that California in the USA, where it's forever sunny and everyone's always on the beach; no, it was just a local team, from wet, windy North Yorkshire! The man spoke to my dad and invited me to come down for Saturday morning training sessions. That sounded great, except for one thing: **he wanted me to train with their girls' team**.

ANOTHER GIRLS' TEAM – DID I HAVE TO?

In my head, I was thinking it would be just like the Middlesbrough Academy all over again.

'Dad, I want to go and play with the boys instead!' I said as I sat there crying in the car. I always played with the boys; that was what I was used to. So when we arrived for my first session with the California team, my dad went over to speak to the coach, and he agreed to let me train with the boys at first, just to build up my confidence. But in the end, I settled in so well that I played for the boys' team for two whole years!

When I did eventually join the California girls' team later, it turned out that I had been **worrying over nothing**. They were all very friendly and welcomed me into the group straight away. But still, I really loved my time with the California boys too. I also developed a lot as a player there, **getting stuck in and holding my own, showing my fighting spirit as well as my skill.**

My teammates never said anything about me being a girl, but when I walked out on to the pitch to play in league matches, sometimes opposition players or their parents would laugh and make comments about me.

GET READY TO ROAR ACTIVITY

Have you ever heard anyone laugh at you or make comments about you? If so, what did you do about it?

A) Reacted angrily

B) Gave up on doing what you wanted to do

C) Just ignored it

D) Reported it to a responsible adult

I hope your answer wasn't a) or b) – it's important to keep going; **calmly follow your path!** If you do hear someone say something that's a little bit mean, my advice would be **c) – try to ignore it and prove them wrong on the pitch**. But if it's something serious like racism or discrimination, then definitely **d) – you've got to report it to a referee or coach straight away**.

OR have you ever overheard someone else being laughed at or bullied? If so, what did you do about it?

A) Just stood back and kept quiet

B) Supported the person who was being laughed at

C) Joined in with the laughing

The answer I'm hoping for is . . . b)! I know it's not always easy to be brave and speak up, especially if there is a big group of bullies. But there are other things you can do to support people too – such as checking in with them, showing them friendship or, again, if it's really bad, reporting to an adult.

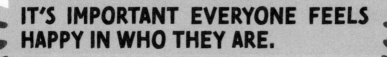

IT'S IMPORTANT EVERYONE FEELS HAPPY IN WHO THEY ARE.

I never let any of that noise bother me, though, because I was happy in who I was, doing what I wanted to do.

'JUST LET YOUR FOOTBALL DO THE TALKING'

– that's what my dad always said to me, and so that's what I always did.

In fact, one of his favourite memories is me going in for a 50-50 challenge against the biggest boy on the pitch. Suddenly, he heard a scream and his first thought was, 'Oh no, Beth must be hurt!' But no, I jumped back up and dribbled away with the ball, while the big boy was still lying there on the floor!

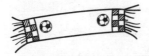

Like me, lots of kids love sports when they're really young, but often they give up when they get a bit older. **Sport is suddenly not seen as 'cool' any more**, and so sometimes people stop doing it and follow the crowd. **I think that's such a shame, don't you?** This is why I want you to think about what makes you happy and do those things, no matter what your friends or everyone else is getting up to.

I never lost my love of sport, and football in particular. I was

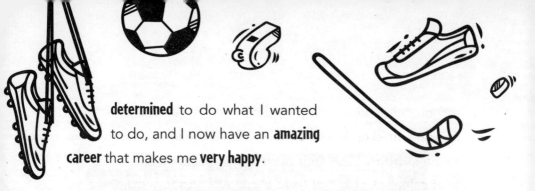

determined to do what I wanted to do, and I now have an **amazing career** that makes me **very happy**.

It helped that at my secondary school, I was never seen as weird or strange for playing sport. Everyone did it. A lot of my friends, however, were more interested in hockey and cross country. I spent **AGES** trying to persuade them to form a girls' school football team with me, telling them, 'All you have to do is stand there on the pitch and I'll do all the running!' But sadly, even that didn't work.

Luckily, things have changed a lot since then. Now that the game is getting really popular, more schools are forming girls' football teams. But what about **YOUR** favourite sport? Does your school already have a team you can join? If not, then **get your friends together and talk to a teacher about it**!

Despite not playing the game in school, I was still happy in my own football world outside of school, firing my way through the Middlesbrough Centre of Excellence. My friends loved buying new clothes to wear out at the weekend, and don't get me wrong, I enjoyed that too, but my favourite shopping trips were going with my dad to buy new football boots. Before every new season, we would make an exciting day out of it. I **LOVED** walking into our local sports shop, going upstairs to the boot section, and then trying on different styles and sizes, even though I often ended up choosing the same ones as before. My very first boots had been plain black and cost 50p from a car boot sale. But now that I was a goal-scoring forward, I had my eyes on the brightest pair in the shop, which probably weren't the cheapest either. **Sorry, Dad, but it was worth it in the end!**

Hero: Thierry Henry

Thierry Henry is **one of the greatest strikers of all time**. With his country, France, he won the 1998 World Cup and Euro 2000, and he also led his English club, Arsenal, to two Premier League titles and two FA Cup trophies in the early 2000s.

Seriously, what a player! I was never allowed to have an Henry shirt, though, and there was a very good reason for that – my family and I are all Manchester United fans!

But even though he didn't play for 'our team', growing up, I loved everything about Henry: **the goals, the skills, the speed, the celebrations**, but most of all, I loved his **calm and class**. In goal-scoring situations where other people might panic, he was always so chilled. He knew what he was doing, and he just did it. **BANG! . . . GOAL!**

As a striker myself, I wanted to be a hero like Henry. In games, whenever I got a chance to score, I always tried to copy his cool, calm finishing. And most of the time, it worked!

BETH'S TOP THREE FAVOURITE BOOTS:

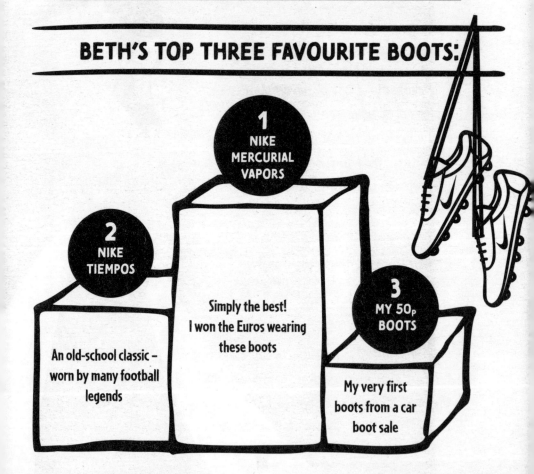

1
NIKE MERCURIAL VAPORS

Simply the best! I won the Euros wearing these boots

2
NIKE TIEMPOS

An old-school classic – worn by many football legends

3
MY 50p BOOTS

My very first boots from a car boot sale

BETH'S PRE-CHAPTER WARM-UP: REACH FOR THE STARS

This chapter is all about dreaming big, so to kick things off, I want you to . . . Reach for the stars! This stretch is good for:

- ✓ Helping posture and balance
- ✓ Relieving achy and tight muscles
- ✓ Warming up/waking up the body

WHAT TO DO: From a standing position, reach your arms up as high as you can. Then, try again while standing on your tiptoes.

EXTRA TIME: After reaching up for the stars, try reaching out to your left and then your right.

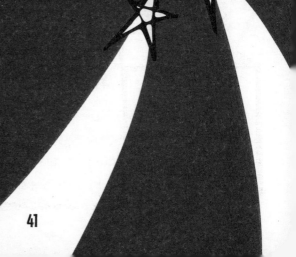

CHAPTER THREE

DREAM BIG AND SET YOUR SUPERSTAR GOALS

HAVING FUN SO FAR? I hope so; I definitely am. Now let's look to the future. I have a big question to ask **YOU**:

WHAT'S YOUR ULTIMATE DREAM?

If you close your eyes and think positively, what amazing things do you picture yourself doing?

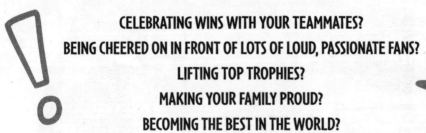

CELEBRATING WINS WITH YOUR TEAMMATES?
BEING CHEERED ON IN FRONT OF LOTS OF LOUD, PASSIONATE FANS?
LIFTING TOP TROPHIES?
MAKING YOUR FAMILY PROUD?
BECOMING THE BEST IN THE WORLD?

The answer I'm looking for is: all of those and more! My aim in this chapter is to encourage you to aim as high as possible, as high as **YOU** want to go in your particular sport, and in life too. Why? Well, let me start with a fact that might surprise some of you:

As a kid, I **never really dreamed** of being a professional footballer.

Growing up, I got into football because I loved the game, not because I wanted to do it as a job in the future. To be honest, that idea hardly crossed my mind, even when I was doing well and scoring lots of goals at Middlesbrough.

So what job did I dream of doing instead?

BETH'S TOP THREE CHILDHOOD DREAM JOBS:

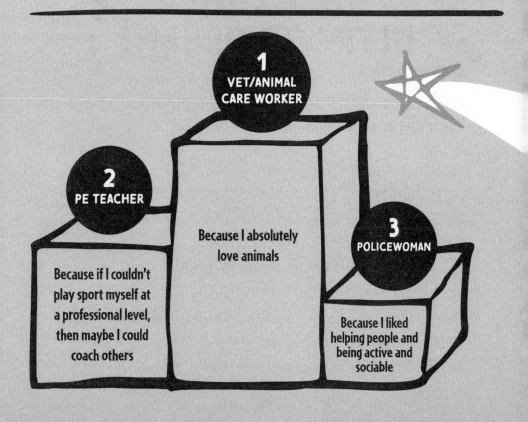

1
VET/ANIMAL CARE WORKER

2
PE TEACHER

3
POLICEWOMAN

Because I absolutely love animals

Because if I couldn't play sport myself at a professional level, then maybe I could coach others

Because I liked helping people and being active and sociable

When I was really young, I loved looking after animals, whether they were the plastic horses on my little animal farm toy set or my real-life pets: my rabbit, Beethoven (named after the film about the dog – if you haven't seen it, go watch it now; it's amazing!), and my dog, Jess. Even now, twenty years later, I'd still love to open my own animal sanctuary one day. I've even got a name for it already: Meado Manor! **What do you think?**

Anyway, sorry, I'm getting carried away – let's get back to sport. As I got older, I thought about doing other jobs, but never becoming a professional footballer.

WHY NOT? I wanted to play the sport I loved, of course, but doing it full-time as a proper paid job just didn't seem realistic for me as a girl.

Playing football for famous teams in famous stadiums in front of big crowds? That was something that I saw lots of men like **David Beckham** and **Wayne Rooney** do every week on TV. But women? No, they never seemed to get that same opportunity, and if I couldn't see it, how was I supposed to be it?

I knew the names of a few female footballers – **Kelly Smith**, **Rachel Yankey**, **Alex Scott** – but that was about it. When I first joined Middlesbrough in 2005, aged nine, there was no Women's

Super League (WSL), no big sponsorship deals and definitely no Lionesses selling out Wembley in less than twenty-four hours.

It was only when I was about sixteen or seventeen, after I'd signed for Sunderland, that being a professional footballer became a more realistic goal. But even then, in 2011, most of the female footballers I played with still weren't fully professional. They had to have other part-time jobs too, like sports coaching (**Jill Scott**), or working in a pizza place (**Lucy Bronze**) or a pub (me!).

Luckily, the women's game has come a long way in the years since then, and the impact of England winning the Euros in 2022 has been incredible to see. It's so nice to know that our achievement has helped to raise the profile of women's football in this country and around the world people are taking the women's game seriously. At **Arsenal**, we're now playing regularly at the Emirates Stadium in front of forty or **FIFTY**

THOUSAND FANS, whereas our normal stadium only holds three thousand. Now that's what I call **progress**!

And the girls' game has changed a lot too. If you're an experienced young female player, there are better academies, coaches and training facilities than when I was young. And if you're a beginner, there are more teams, more players and more ways to play than ever. I think it's so important to make getting into sport as easy as possible.

If I could, I would love to time-travel and be a kid again now, because there are so many **great female sporting role models** to look up to.

> 'WHOEVER YOU ARE, YOU CAN SEE IT AND SO YOU CAN BE IT.'

I hope that the path to playing top-level sport is now much clearer for everyone. So **my** main message to you, reader, is this:

DREAM BIG, REALLY, REALLY BIG
– RIGHT FROM THE BEGINNING.

What would be **YOUR** ultimate sporting dream? You can go **big** and **ambitious** if you like – perhaps you want to be the best swimmer in the world! Or you can keep it simple – perhaps your sporting dream is to find a fun and supportive netball team that you can win the local league with. Or maybe you love running and want to be the fastest in your school.

Now have a think about a big life dream outside of sport too. I love sport but as I said earlier, I also love animals and a dream of mine is to open up my own animal sanctuary in the future. What about you – what would be your ultimate dream **outside of sport**? Again, you can go big and ambitious with this!

BIG DREAM, SMALLER GOALS

Once you've decided on your ultimate dreams on and off the pitch, the next step is setting out your path to get there. Because, **WARNING**: you're not going to achieve your biggest goal straight away. If it was that easy, it wouldn't be much of a challenge, would it? Your **ultimate dream** should be something that takes time and lots of **hard work** and **dedication**, so it's important to give yourself stepping stones to follow along the journey. Think of it like a road map to **success**.

Like I said before, as a young player, I couldn't picture myself playing professional football, but that doesn't mean I wasn't still ambitious and determined. I had my sporting dreams; it's just that instead of saying I wanted to play for a big club like Arsenal in front of fifty thousand fans at the Emirates **(TICK!)** ✔ or win the Women's Euros with England and finish as top scorer **(TICK!)**, I was working towards smaller goals that felt more achievable:

1) To keep improving each week, month and year

AND

2) To one day play at the highest level possible

TICK! ✔ **TICK!** ✔ Whether I was playing for California or Middlesbrough, I was always competitive and always committed to becoming a **better player**. As I worked my way up through the Middlesbrough Centre of Excellence – Under-13s,

Under-14s, Under-15s – I developed a reputation as a really **sharp-shooting striker**. Each year, my aim was to score more goals than I had the previous season, and usually I succeeded.

It's the same off the pitch too. If you want to get good at something, it can feel daunting at first, until you break it down into **smaller, more achievable goals**. For example, at school, maths was never my strongest subject. Me and numbers just don't go well together, but I was determined to go to university, so I needed to pass my maths GCSE. But how was I going to do that? By working day by day, week by week, towards that bigger target: doing extra practice at home, taking after-school classes, completing online quizzes . . .

On the day we got our results, I was so nervous, but I opened up the envelope and . . . **I'd got a good grade**! Mum and I both burst out crying because I had worked so hard, step by step, to achieve what I wanted.

SO WHAT ABOUT YOU? What are you aiming to achieve this year, and what about next year? You see, as you work towards your ultimate dreams on and off the pitch, you're going to need to set yourself a range of different goals, to help keep you motivated:

SHORT TERM – something that you could achieve in a week, e.g. working on a weakness

MID TERM – something that might take a bit longer, maybe even a few months, e.g. mastering a new skill

LONG TERM – anything that will take longer than three months to achieve, e.g. winning a big competition or becoming the best player in the entire world!

Time to have a go at setting your own **SUPERSTAR GOALS**!

GET READY TO ROAR ACTIVITY

I want you to write down **three goals for yourself**: one short term, one mid term, and one long term. Then, write down **three goals for your ultimate dream** outside of sport too. If you like, you could then put them up on your bedroom wall to remind yourself!

But as you set off chasing your big dreams and smaller goals, please don't forget one very important thing that we talked about in chapters one and two: **FUN**! You've got to enjoy yourself, otherwise what's the point?

The balance between aiming high and having fun can be hard to get right. Sometimes, we can get so focused on achieving something big that we forget why we fell in love with that thing in the first place. That's what happened to me a few years ago, as you'll read about more in chapter seven. After a series of setbacks, I **lost my love of the game** for a little while, and it was only once I went back to enjoying football that I found my top form again.

So even now, after winning the **WSL title with Arsenal** and the **Euros with England**, I still make sure to remind myself of the reasons why I got into football in the first place:

FREEDOM, FUN, GOALS, AND FRIENDSHIPS,

rather than **FAME, MONEY, GLORY, AND FANCY CARS**.

GET READY TO ROAR ACTIVITY

Have a think about why you fell in love with your sport in the first place. Was it a particular player who inspired you, a friend or a coach, or maybe even just a feeling? Or write down some reasons for your ultimate dream outside of sport too. **Sometimes, it's just good to remind yourself!**

It doesn't matter where you're from or what you want to do, I believe **EVERYONE SHOULD DREAM BIG**. Anything is possible with enough hard work, talent and belief. So, go on:

DREAM **BIG**,

SET YOUR SMALLER GOALS ALONG THE WAY,

AND DON'T FORGET TO **HAVE FUN!**

Hero: Kelly Smith

My two biggest childhood football heroes, **Thierry Henry** and **Kelly Smith**, both played for Arsenal, the club that I now play for. Funny, eh? It really was meant to be!

If you don't already know about Kelly, you need to go and look her up. Seriously, **she's one of the best strikers in the history of the women's game**, and an absolute England **legend**. Between 1995 and 2014, she scored 46 goals in 117 games for the Lionesses, including four at the 2007 FIFA World Cup.

My earliest experience of women's football was going with Dad to watch Kelly play for Arsenal against Leeds Carnegie. I was so excited about seeing my hero play, but we got stuck in traffic and arrived fifteen minutes late. By the time we finally took our seats and looked out at the pitch, Kelly was nowhere to be seen. Where was she? It turned out she'd already scored two goals and then been sent off!

After the match, all of the Arsenal players came over to our side of the pitch to sign autographs, including Kelly. 'Go and speak to her – she's just over there!' Dad told me, but I was feeling shy, so in the end he had to come with me. Although she was really friendly and signed my shirt, I was still too nervous to say much back.

Now, when I see young girls getting excited about meeting me, I find it weird that I'm that person, but I can also understand it because once upon a time that was me with Kelly Smith. Meeting your heroes is a **MASSIVE, INSPIRING MOMENT**, and hey, you never know what it might lead to!

BETH'S PRE-CHAPTER WARM-UP: THE BALLOON BASH

I hope you're in the mood to party because it's time for a game I like to call . . . the balloon bash! It's good for:

- ✓ Co-ordination
- ✓ Ball control
- ✓ Concentration

WHAT TO DO: Blow up a balloon and bat it up in the air, using your hand or any other part of your body.

YOUR CHALLENGE: Keep the balloon in the air for one minute. You can hit it as hard and high as you like, but just don't let it drop to the floor!

EXTRA TIME: Too easy? You could try doing it as a team with your friends for five minutes, or try using only one hand, or even harder, only one foot.

CHAPTER FOUR

DON'T STAY IN THE SHALLOW END (FOR EVER)

We all like to feel safe and comfortable, don't we? Sheltering indoors when it's pouring with rain outside, getting a great big hug from a grown-up we love when we're upset or scared, snuggling under the duvet to watch a film on a freezing cold winter's day . . .

Most of the time, somewhere safe and comfortable is the best place to be, but not always. Sometimes we can get **TOO** comfortable in the environment we're in, and that can hold us back and get in the way of us achieving our **dreams**.

I'll use swimming as an example. I want you to start by thinking back to when you first learned to swim at your local pool – for me, that's Loftus Leisure Centre. To be honest, I can't really remember much about the pool itself; my main focus was the vending machine and what I was going to eat afterwards!

But all pools have at least two things in common:

a) **A shallow end**

and

b) **A deep(er) end**

When you first learn to swim, you start off in the shallow end because that's a **much safer place to be**. As a beginner, you don't want to feel like you're **out of your depth**.

But if you want to push on and become a good swimmer, doing full lengths of the pool, then eventually you're going to have to **BE BRAVE**. You're going to have to take a deep breath, leave the shallow end behind, and go where your feet don't touch the bottom.

I remember some kids in my swim class wanted to push on towards the deep end as quickly as possible, but others stayed in the shallow end for longer, thinking, 'What's the rush? The more challenging bit can wait. I'm happy right here for now.'

Which type of character are you – would you stay or would you go, go, go?

I was definitely a **COMFORT ZONE KID**. What I mean by that is that I preferred to stay in a place where I felt safe and comfortable. As a country girl who was very close to my family, I absolutely hated new environments and it always took me a long time to adapt. Although I've got better at it over the years, it's something I'm still working on. That's why I cried at every training session when I first moved to Middlesbrough, and that's why my coaches there were always saying in their end-of-season reports,

'BETH – VERY GOOD PLAYER BUT NEEDS TO PUSH HERSELF HARDER.'

When I was twelve, I was invited along to a county/regional training camp that was taking place in Hull. Sounds fun, right? Well, I wasn't so sure about that. I would be playing with the best young footballers from all over Yorkshire, who I didn't know, and doing football sessions that I wasn't familiar with. Did I definitely want to do this? What was the rush? I was happy where I was at Middlesbrough for now . . .

But luckily with a bit of friendly **encouragement** from my parents, I decided to be brave and do it. Dad took me down, and I remember feeling **very nervous** during the training drills in the morning. I didn't really get into it until the afternoon, when the proper games began. That was more like it! Now I was excited and up for it, and I ended up scoring a hat-trick in one of the matches.

'WHERE HAS THIS GIRL BEEN?!' THE COACHES WONDERED.

'HOW HAVE WE NOT KNOWN ABOUT HER?'

After that, there was **good news** and **bad news**. Thanks to my goals, I was through to the next stage, but things were about to get even scarier. I was off to an England national under-16s training camp. **GULP!**

Not only would the level be even higher, but I would also have to be away from home for a night. **WOAH**, talk about leaving my comfort zone! Couldn't I just stay where I was in the shallow end?

NO! The first camp I went to was down in Loughborough, and I didn't know anyone there, except for one of my Middlesbrough teammates. I loved the football side of things, but I found being away from home and my family really hard. Instead of sleeping, **I cried all night long**, which must have been annoying for my roommate. **SORRY, BETH ENGLAND!** (Luckily she forgave me – she's one of my good friends and we still play football together – for England!)

GET READY TO ROAR ACTIVITY

Can you think of any times in your own life where you've stayed too long in the shallow end? If so, write down what it was that worried you and made you want to stay in your comfort zone. What was it that you were most afraid of? And if you did push yourself forward, how did it feel?

Usually **the fear of something is much worse than the reality**. I was scared of trying something new, but when I went to the training camp in Hull, not only did I have fun, I got selected for the England Under-16s! I had nothing to worry about at all. Write down some ways you can push yourself forward in the future and talk it through with someone you trust.

If, like me, you find it hard to adapt to new environments, then my top tip for you is this:

DON'T BE AFRAID TO TALK ABOUT IT.

SPEAK OUT and **SHARE YOUR FEELINGS** with others rather than keeping them bottled up inside. Whether it's a teammate, a teacher, a friend or a family member, they can help to put your worries into perspective and hopefully make things easier.

As you chase your individual dreams, I think it's so important to have support around you. Thankfully, I had two people by my side who always believed in me and knew what was best for me.

Heroes: Mum and Dad

If it wasn't for my parents, I wouldn't be a professional footballer – it's as simple as that, really.

I WOULD **NEVER** BE WHERE I AM WITHOUT THEM.

I have **so much to thank them for**: all the hours spent driving me to and from matches, all the new kits and boots they bought and, most importantly, all the times when they encouraged me to go beyond my comfort zone.

As a kid, I didn't really have the **self-belief** to push myself on the football pitch. It can be hard at a young age to take a leap into the unknown. On my own, I'm really not sure I would have gone on to **fulfil my potential**, but luckily, I had Mum and Dad. They always believed in me and so they **pushed me to keep testing myself at the highest level possible**. When I say they pushed me, they didn't force me to play; they were just trying to help me become a better player. They knew I would thank them for it in the end, and I have, many times – **I PROMISE**!

The night before an England youth camp, I would always get really upset and say I didn't want to go.

'Well, if you're going to be like this then there's no point you playing football,' Dad would often say to me.

'Fine, I won't play football then,' I would reply grumpily, and to prove it, I sometimes threw my England kit in the bin!

But Dad knew me; he knew that I didn't mean it. I was just being stubborn, and **surprise, surprise**, a few minutes later I would get my kit back out of the bin and carry on with football. I loved the game way too much to give up.

Mum knew that too. The night before England camps, she would take me out for a walk to calm me down. 'You're going to be OK,' she'd tell me. 'You're off to play football, something that you love. You'll be back here in no time.'

She was right, of course. It was the thought of going that was always the worst part for me. Each time, I would leave home in tears, but once I played football, **I was fine**.

Fast forward ten years and Mum and Dad were there at Wembley as England won the Euros and I won the **Best Player** and **Top Goal Scorer awards**, which I later gave to them. I was so glad to be able to share it with them after everything they've done for me. As my parents knew all along, **IT HAD ALL BEEN WORTH IT!**

So yes, my parents were **very important** in helping me move on out of the shallow end, but they weren't the only ones. I also had two coaches who pushed me massively in my early football years.

The first was **Andy Cook at Middlesbrough**. He believed in me from the beginning, always challenging me to score more goals and helping me practise my technique, even after training finished. He had a huge influence on me.

Then, aged sixteen, I was approaching the end of my spell at the Centre of Excellence when suddenly the rules changed and the club added a new under-17s team. At the time, I was thinking about going to Sunderland to continue my career at senior level. It was a bigger club with a **brilliant reputation** for developing young players. England legends **Steph Houghton**, **Jill Scott**, **Lucy Bronze** – they had all started off at Sunderland.

But suddenly I didn't have to move any more.

HURRAY, I COULD STAY IN MY COMFORT ZONE!

Well, for another year, anyway. Yes, that 'I'm happy right here for now' feeling kicked in again.

Middlesbrough wanted me to stay too, but I had to do what was best for me. It took me a while to decide whether to stay or go. But eventually I realised I had gone as far as I could go at Middlesbrough. To get better, and fulfil my potential, I needed a new challenge. Andy supported me in my decision, and he's been cheering me on ever since!

THANKS, ANDY!

Who knows what might have happened if I hadn't moved. Maybe I would still have become a top professional footballer anyway, but maybe I wouldn't have made it. One thing's for sure, though: **taking that leap and signing for Sunderland pushed me on to become the player that I am now**.

The other coach who had a big impact on me was the **Sunderland manager, Mick Mulhern**. When I still wasn't sure if I wanted to sign for the club or not, he was great and took the time to speak to me properly. According to Dad, he even drove to meet us in a Morrisons car park once, midway between Sunderland and where we lived. I don't remember the conversation at all, but that's probably because I was being stubborn again. Trying something scary and new?

NO THANKS, NOT LISTENING!

Mick didn't give up on me, though. 'Just come up for a training session,' he suggested, 'and see how you feel. No pressure either way. Then you can decide and go from there.'

Eventually I said yes, and surprise, surprise – I loved it at Sunderland! My biggest worries were answered straight away:

WOULD I FIT IN? Yes, the other girls made me feel really welcome, especially the captain, **Steph Bannon**. She was unbelievable with me, and we're still close friends to this day.

WAS I GOOD ENOUGH? Yes, and it was exactly the new challenge that I needed.

'I WANT TO STAY HERE!' I TOLD MUM AND DAD AFTER THAT FIRST SESSION.

'I WANT TO PLAY FOR THIS TEAM.'

From that moment on, I never looked back. Signing for Sunderland was the best decision I've ever made, and Mick showed so much belief in me, right from the start. Even though I was still only sixteen, he put me into the women's team immediately, and that gave me **so much confidence** to go forward and grow as a player. Sometimes, that extra bit of belief is all you need to **GO, GO, GO**!

In my first year, I scored 23 goals in 23 games,

then in my second, I scored 30 in 28.

Two seasons, two Golden Boot awards – not bad, eh? And there would be more of those to come. But if I hadn't taken the leap to test myself at Sunderland, I would never have developed in the way that I have.

Not everyone's lucky enough to have the full backing and support of a mum and dad like I did, or coaches who can fill you with confidence. But there will always be people who are your champions!

GET READY TO ROAR ACTIVITY

Have a think about the people who are always there for you, who make you **happy** and **support** you in what you do. Perhaps it's your best friend, a teacher, a coach, a family member or even your pet. Those people (or animals!) who make you feel safe and supported and will always have your back.

These people are your **CHAMPIONS**!

Write down their names and remember, they are there when you need them, to help you swim fast and strong in the deep end and go on to achieve your dreams.

So far in this chapter, I've been focusing on the **world of sport**, but I think we all have our comfort zones in other areas of life too.

You might think:

'WHAT'S THE RUSH? I'M HAPPY RIGHT HERE FOR NOW.'

But whatever you want to do, whether it's becoming an astronaut or getting really good at art, you have to **keep pushing yourself forward** and say **YES** to opportunities that come your way.

No matter what your dreams are, remember:

AS SAFE AND COMFORTABLE AS IT MIGHT FEEL, DON'T STAY IN THE SHALLOW END FOR EVER.

ALWAYS BELIEVE IN YOURSELF, IN THE ABILITY THAT YOU HAVE, AND PUSH YOURSELF TO GO A BIT FURTHER, TO REACH THAT NEXT LEVEL.

ANYTHING IS POSSIBLE.

BETH'S TOP THREE FAVOURITE FOOTBALL PITCHES/STADIUMS:

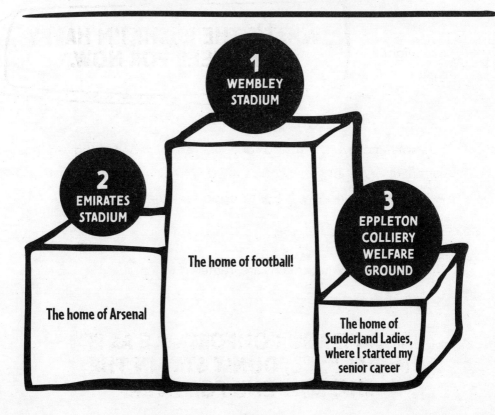

1 WEMBLEY STADIUM
The home of football!

2 EMIRATES STADIUM
The home of Arsenal

3 EPPLETON COLLIERY WELFARE GROUND
The home of Sunderland Ladies, where I started my senior career

BETH'S PRE-CHAPTER WARM-UP: STEP IN, STEP OUT

This chapter is all about taking things step by step, so here's an activity called . . . Step in, step out! It's good for:

- ✓ Co-ordination
- ✓ Concentration
- ✓ Speed
- ✓ Agility

WHAT TO DO: Using chalk, draw a circle on the ground. Then step in to the circle, one foot at a time, and then out again, one foot at a time. They've got to be steps; no jumping allowed!

YOUR CHALLENGE: Step in and out of the circle as many times as you can in sixty seconds.

EXTRA TIME: Try stepping in and out of the circle in different directions: left, right, forwards, backwards.

TWIST IT UP: Why not try throwing a ball to someone in the circle instead? See how many you can do in sixty seconds and then move further away and try again.

CHAPTER FIVE

TAKE THINGS ONE STEP AT A TIME

For the last two chapters, we've been **ZOOMING** ahead towards the future at record-breaking speed, so now let's slow things down a bit, catch our breath and **take our time**.

Don't worry, I still want you to **dream big** and **step out of your comfort zone**, but I want you to move at your own pace.

Have you ever heard the tale of the tortoise and the hare? I'm sure you have, but let me remind you of the details. In the story, the hare mocks the tortoise for being slow, so the tortoise challenges him to a race. Of course, the hare rushes out in front because he's a lot faster, but he's so far ahead that he decides to take a nap. While he sleeps, the tortoise keeps going at his own speed until eventually he overtakes the hare. And so slow and steady wins the race.

HURRAY!

WHAT ABOUT YOU? Would you say you're more of a tortoise, progressing slowly and carefully step by step, or a hare, racing ahead without really thinking things through?

I'd say I'm probably somewhere in between the tortoise and the hare, but I definitely **don't believe in rushing into things**, especially not when it comes to sport.

'BE NOT AFRAID OF GROWING SLOWLY, BE AFRAID ONLY OF STANDING STILL'
– THAT'S A CHINESE PROVERB I CAN RELATE TO.

Instead of hurrying straight from beginner to the best as fast as you can, it's important to **TAKE THINGS ONE STEP AT A TIME**.

This means avoiding putting too much pressure on yourself. Instead, you find the right amount of pressure that works for **YOU**.

To show you what I mean, I want to tell you a story about my move from Sunderland to Arsenal.

The story starts in 2014, my third year at Sunderland and the first year of the Women's Super League 2 (WSL2). For once, I didn't need time to adapt to a new environment. I finished the season with 13 goals in 15 games, and we finished two points ahead of Doncaster Belles at the top of the table.

HURRAY, WE HAD WON THE LEAGUE! And that wasn't all; we had also been promoted to the WSL. Next season, Sunderland would be taking on the biggest teams in England: Liverpool, Chelsea, Manchester City . . .

. . . and Arsenal. They were a club I already loved because of my two childhood heroes, **Kelly Smith** and **Thierry Henry**, and a club that I had always wanted to play for. And now, amazingly, their manager, **Pedro Martínez Losa**, was interested in signing me. Really? Wow! I couldn't believe it.

My first thought was **'Great, let's go!'**

But luckily I slowed down to think things through.

Wait a minute – was it the right time for me to make my dream move?

I thought about it and I decided to say no to Arsenal.

YEP, I SAID NO TO MY DREAM TEAM.

Do you think that sounds crazy?!

I promise, I did have my reasons:

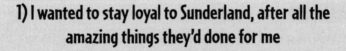

1) I wanted to stay loyal to Sunderland, after all the amazing things they'd done for me

2) I wanted to stay at Teesside University and finish my degree in sports development

But the biggest reason of all was this:

3) I wanted to keep taking things one step at a time

Don't get me wrong – as we talked about in the last chapter, it is important to leave your comfort zone behind and keep pushing forward, but you want to do it when the timing is right. Think of yourself as a plant growing in a greenhouse. You get taller and taller until eventually, you hit the ceiling and you can't go any further. **What now? Time to move!** At Middlesbrough, I had reached the ceiling and so I'd moved on to a bigger place, Sunderland. At Sunderland, I knew I was getting close to the ceiling, but I still had enough room left to grow, and one more step to take: **into the WSL**!

From the Middlesbrough Centre of Excellence, I had moved up to the Sunderland senior team and then starred in the WSL2. So now, before I joined a big club like Arsenal, I wanted to gain some WSL experience with Sunderland and prove myself at the highest level.

See, my decision makes sense now, doesn't it? It was actually the first time that Mum, Dad and I all agreed on something in my football career!

Step by step, I had been working towards my ultimate sporting dream for years, so why would I suddenly now start rushing? I was moving at my own pace. Plus, what if I went to Arsenal and just sat on the bench all season? No thanks! I was still only nineteen and I wanted to be playing every week. So I decided to stay at Sunderland for another season.

It's your life and you've got to do what feels right for you.

What would you have done in my position at Sunderland: stay or go?

Looking back, it was a risky move to say 'not now' to Arsenal, but luckily, that first WSL season went well for me. Really well, actually. Sunderland finished in fourth place and I finished as the top scorer in the league, with 12 goals in 14 games.

Prove myself in the WSL – **TICK!** ✔

Arsenal didn't go away. A year later, they came back to try and sign me again, and this time, I said yes. As the famous saying goes,

'GOOD THINGS COME TO THOSE WHO WAIT.'

The timing was now right for me to take the next step in my football journey.

Well, sort of. **Unfortunately**, when I signed for the club in January 2017, I had just picked up an ankle injury playing for the England Under-23s. That made settling in much harder for me because football has always been my favourite way to escape and have fun. Without that, what was I supposed to do with myself? Every morning, I went into the Arsenal training ground for physio sessions, but then what about the afternoon and the evening? **Suddenly, I had a lot of time to fill.**

I couldn't get comfortable on the pitch because I was injured, and at first, I couldn't get comfortable off it either. I felt lost in a new city, a new club, a new environment. It was like my early struggles with Middlesbrough and England Under-16s all over again. The days felt so long and I remember many tearful phone calls with Mum where I told her I wanted to come home.

'No, no, you're going to be just fine,' she'd tell me calmly, breaking my day down into smaller, more manageable bits. **'Make yourself some food, then go out and get some fresh air...'**

In the end, Mum came down to London and brought the comfort of home to me instead. She also brought me a gift that will always mean so much to me. **It's a pebble from my favourite beach back home, at Runswick Bay**, and a local artist had decorated it with five short, simple, but very wise words:

ONE STEP
AT A TIME

It really was the perfect message for me at that moment in my life. I needed to hear it, and maybe so might you at some point in your sporting journey.

Some things take time, and that's **OK**. We all have our own speeds and our journeys. If you find yourself struggling as you chase your dream, don't hide away and give up. Stick with it, stay consistent, slow and steady, and surround yourself with supportive champions, as we mentioned in the last chapter, as well as the things that make you happy. **'Comfort blankets'** are what I like to call them. Eventually, you'll get to where you want to go, bit by bit, step by step . . .

BETH'S TOP THREE COMFORT BLANKETS:

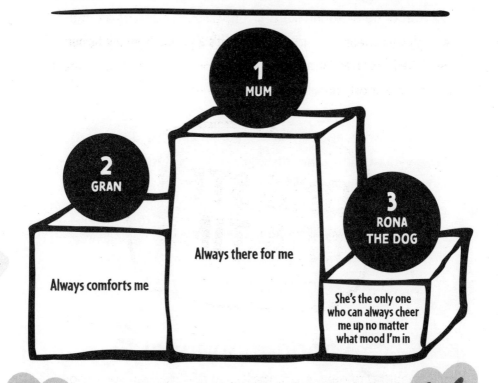

1
MUM

2
GRAN

3
RONA
THE DOG

Always there for me

Always comforts me

She's the only one who can always cheer me up no matter what mood I'm in

GET READY TO ROAR ACTIVITY

1) **What about you** – what would your top three comfort blankets be? Have a go at writing a list like mine.

2) If you could write down one message to help motivate yourself during tough times, what would it be? Why not try and find a big stone you can write it on, or design a poster and stick it on your wall? **Go on, get creative!**

After about a month at Arsenal, I got myself into a good routine and started to feel happier and more at home. Then, soon, I was able to start playing football again, and that made everything so much better. **Hurray, I was back!**

For a little while, anyway. But remember what I said earlier about taking your time and not rushing into things? **Well, unfortunately, I forgot to follow my own advice.** After a few good training sessions, I got a bit carried away and decided I was ready to push on and prove myself at my new club. I was so excited and impatient that I raced in for a 50-50 challenge with the goalkeeper. The keeper got to the ball first and I flew over the top of her, breaking my collarbone.

NOOOOOOOOOOOOO!

It was another six frustrating weeks without football for me. So yes, let that be a lesson to you (and me!): in both good times and bad times, it's always best to take things one step at a time!

As you chase a big dream, it's so easy to rush ahead and put too much pressure on yourself. **But instead of being a hare, try being a bit more tortoise.** Go at your own pace, celebrate your little victories and try not to keep comparing yourself to others around you. **Every journey is different, so be kind to yourself and enjoy each step of the adventure.**

Hero: Jordan Nobbs

As well as being an amazing footballer, Jordan is also one of my **best friends**. When I first arrived at Arsenal, I moved into a house with Jordan and two other players: **Katie McCabe** and **Jemma Rose**. I already knew all about her talent on the pitch because she had made the same journey as me years earlier, from Sunderland to Arsenal.

Off the pitch, we quickly became good friends and she really helped me to settle in during those early injured days when I had nothing else to do. She could see that I was struggling, and so she'd often take me for a chat or have dinner with me. They were small things for her, but they made a massive difference to me. Jordan's from up north like me, so being around her felt comfortable and familiar. She was a piece of home, away from home, and she could understand what I was going through. Her main advice was the same as Mum's: **TAKE THINGS ONE STEP AT A TIME.**

Since then, Jordan and I have travelled all over the world together, with Arsenal and England, experiencing lots of highs and lots of lows. But the important thing is that we're always there for each other. We all need friends like Jordan in our lives.

HALF-TIME

OK, it's time to take a quick pause and peek behind the scenes. Ever wondered what a professional footballer does during that fifteen-minute break between the first and second half? **WELL, LET ME TELL YOU!**

1) After walking off the pitch, we head straight into the changing room, where we have two or three minutes to talk to our teammates about the performance so far. **What do we need to keep doing? What could we do better?**

2) Then the manager comes in with his analysis team to deliver the **half-time team talk**. Usually, they'll put video clips from the first half up on a big screen for us to watch and learn from.

3) While we're listening to the manager's message, we're also **refuelling with caffeine and carbohydrate gels** to prepare ourselves to go back out and play. Personally, I also drink a special shot at half-time that tastes like vinegar. **EURGH! GROSS.** But it means I'm less likely to get cramp in my legs late in the game.

4) Once the manager's team talk is over, we have a last two or three minutes to go over the **game plan** with each other and share any **final thoughts**. At this stage, if it's been raining, we usually swap our soaking shirts for new dry ones, but if not, no need.

5) Right, time's up – **feeling ready for the second half**?

LET'S GOOOOOOOOO!

BETH'S PRE-CHAPTER WARM-UP: THE KEEPY-UPPIE CHALLENGE

Ready to raise your game? Grab a ball and get your feet moving – it's time for you to take on . . . the keepy-uppie challenge! It's good for:

 Endurance
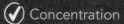 Ball control
 Concentration

WHAT TO DO: Once you're standing in plenty of space, practise flicking the ball up with your feet as many times as you can, without letting it bounce on the ground.

YOUR CHALLENGE: Have ten attempts at seeing how many keepy-uppies you can do in a row. What was your highest score? Now, have another ten attempts – can you beat your previous best?

EXTRA TIME: If you're feeling confident with your feet, try using other parts of your body to keep the ball up too, like your knees, chest, head and shoulders.

TWIST IT UP: If you've got a tennis racket or cricket bat, see how many times you can bounce a tennis ball on that.

CHAPTER SIX

GET INSPIRED AND RAISE YOUR GAME!

'TALENT WILL ONLY GET YOU SO FAR –

HARD WORK WILL GET YOU THE REST OF THE WAY.'

That's what I was told when I was young, and guess what? **It's true!**

Once you reach a high level at something, whether that be in sport or at school, it can sometimes be tempting to think that you've done it, **you've achieved your goal**. At the age of twenty-two, I was playing for Arsenal and England – sounds like I'd 'made it', right?

WRONG! One thing I realised very quickly at Arsenal was that the **hard work never stops**. To stay at the top and make your biggest dreams come true, you've got to keep raising your game every day. You've got to keep:

Listening and learning from others with more experience

and

Adapting and adding to your skillset

LEARNING FROM THOSE AROUND YOU

As a young player, I was lucky enough to be surrounded by talented and experienced teammates. At Sunderland, I had my captain, **Steph Bannon**, plus two England internationals to inspire me: **Kelly McDougall** and **Jermain Defoe**.

Yes, the England striker who had played in the Premier League, the Champions League, the World Cup and the Euros! Jermain was playing for the Sunderland men's team at the time, but he took a real interest in the women's team too, and especially the young striker scoring loads of goals.

'I've heard about you,' he said to me one day in the club canteen we shared with the men's team. **'You're the girl who can score from anywhere on the pitch!'**

WOAH, was this famous footballer really talking to me? The answer was: **YES!** We strikers clicked straight away, and that was the start of a great relationship. In the mornings, we would often sit down together in the club canteen and share stories, experiences and advice.

'This will help you to play football for longer,' Jermain liked to tell me as he handed me a cup of green tea. I did always drink it, but only because it was there waiting for me. I can't say I've had many green teas since – I prefer coffee. **Sorry, Jermain!**

But seriously, it was amazing for me as a young player to be able to sit down and chat with a footballer like Jermain who had already achieved so much in his career. Sadly, we never managed to sort out doing some shooting practice together. That would have been brilliant – **oh well, maybe some day**!

I believe **we can learn so much from the people we play sport with** and the **people who have gone before us**. Here is my three-part superstar mindset, and the people I've learned the most from:

SUPERSTAR MINDSET

1) **HARD WORK:** Whatever your dream, you're going to have to work hard for it, and that **hard work never stops**. When I was at Sunderland, not all of my teammates were full-time professionals. My captain, Steph, for example, was a PE teacher by day and a footballer by night. She would turn up at training after a long day at school, but she never let her tiredness show. Instead, she worked extra hard to keep herself at the highest level, competing in England's top division. For me, as a young player, that was impressive to see, and it's something that I'll always remember.

2) **DEDICATION:** Whatever your dream, **having a positive attitude is essential**. You've got to see every day as a chance to improve. At Arsenal, I was lucky enough to learn from lots of international legends. My first captain at the club was **Alex Scott**, who has since gone on to become a brilliant TV sports presenter and pundit. Even though she was in the last year of her amazing playing career, after getting 140 caps for England, she still led by example every day with her hard work in training. Then my next Arsenal captain was the one and only **Kim Little**.

3) **PERSEVERANCE:** Whatever your dream, you've got to keep working towards it, no matter what. When I became a senior England international in 2018, I had incredible teammates like **Ellen White** and **Jill Scott** to look up to. For years and years, they had put so much heart and energy into wearing the Three Lions shirt. Even after losing in three major tournament semi-finals (the 2015 and 2019 World Cups and Euro 2017) and one final (Euro 2009), they didn't give up. No, **despite the heartbreak** of getting so close to glory so many times, **they had carried on playing for their country**. And not just playing – they still treated every single game as if it was their first for England. It was amazing to see them end their England careers on a high by finally lifting a trophy at Euro 2022.

GET READY TO ROAR ACTIVITY

What have you learned from your teammates or opponents about the sport you love? Make a list and write down the superstar skills they have that make them great.

Hero: KIM LITTLE

With 140 caps for Scotland and over 200 appearances for Arsenal, Kim is an absolute **football legend** and the **ultimate pro**. I've learned so much from her over the last six years, both on and off the pitch. Her focus never drops, not even for a day. She's always pushing herself to improve with the same level of discipline and dedication. In the gym, on the training pitch, in the dressing room, she does everything she can possibly do to be the best because she knows that **even the smallest details can make a massive difference**.

It's so inspiring to see, and it makes you want to be a better player too – the best version of yourself that you can be. **I'M ALWAYS PUSHING MYSELF TO BE MORE LIKE KIM.**

In March 2020, Kim and I got injured at the same time, and our recovery sessions together very quickly turned into a fierce competition. Anything I did in the gym, Kim would be determined to beat it, and then, of course, I would have to beat that, and so on and so on . . . We loved winding each other up, and it worked well because we both returned to the pitch earlier than expected!

It's not just teammates who can inspire you to raise your game either. It can also be heroes who used to play in the past or who play a different sport. Let me give you a couple of quick examples:

1) 1971: THE 'LOST LIONESSES'

Ahead of the Euros, we also had a visit from three of the women from the team known as the **'Lost Lionesses'**. In 1971, they travelled to Mexico to represent England at an unofficial World Cup, and they sat down and spoke to us about their experiences. After the high of playing in front of ninety thousand fans in Mexico and feeling like they were part of something special, they then returned home to England not as heroes but as unknowns, because women were still banned from playing football. **CRAZY, HUH?** Meeting those inspiring women was eye-opening for me. Listening to their stories made me

even more determined to make history and change history at the Euros, and when we met them again afterwards, it was lovely to see how happy they were.

I find it so hard to believe now, but between 1921 and 1971, women weren't allowed to play football in stadiums across England. Yes, the Football Association (the FA) decided that the game was **'QUITE UNSUITABLE FOR FEMALES'** and set out to stop them from playing it. Fifty years without the chance to play the sport you love – **can you imagine how horrible that must have been?** That's why I'm so grateful to all the female footballers, like the 'Lost Lionesses', who fought so hard for the ban to be lifted. Thank you!

2) 2016: THE GB WOMEN'S HOCKEY TEAM

One sporting moment that really inspired me was the **Great Britain women's hockey team winning the Gold Medal at the 2016 Olympics in Rio de Janeiro, Brazil**. I remember watching the final on TV and feeling so emotional afterwards. It was amazing to see those players bounce back from the heartbreak of losing in the semi-finals in 2012 and achieve their ultimate goal at last. Yes, it was a different sport, but it was still the same dream that we England women's footballers were working towards. If the hockey team could do it, **so could we!**

3) 2018: THE ENGLAND WOMEN'S NETBALL TEAM

Another inspiring moment was watching the **England netball team win the Gold Medal at the Commonwealth Games in Australia**. After finishing fourth in 2010, then third in 2014, it was brilliant to see them go all the way to the final and then beat the hosts by one single point. Unbelievable! The team was coached by Tracey Neville, the sister of our former England manager, Phil Neville, and so he got her to come and speak to us before the 2019 World Cup. It was great to hear their story and learn from their experiences.

CAN YOU THINK OF ANY OTHER INSPIRING SPORTING PEOPLE OR MOMENTS TO ADD TO THE LIST YOU'VE ALREADY STARTED?

ADAPTING AND ADDING TO YOUR SKILLSET

I've always found that being around more experienced people is a brilliant way to get **new ideas and new inspiration/motivation**. But that's only the first part of the development process. After that, it's up to **YOU** – you've got to put in the hard work and put all your learning into practice.

In sport, you often hear people talk about someone being 'the complete player' who 'can do it all', but ignore that, because there's no such thing. **There are always new ways you can raise your game**. I like to break it into three:

1. Work hard on your weaknesses

2. Add exciting new powers to your skillset

3. Practise, practise, practise!

In my first season at Arsenal, I played as a central striker, a number 9, like I had at Sunderland, and I did well there, finishing as the team's top scorer. **So far, so good!** I was happy with how things were going, but in the summer of 2017, the club suddenly announced they had signed a new striker, the Dutch superstar **Vivianne Miedema**.

Wait, what? As you can probably guess, I was pretty shocked and confused at first. I thought that was **MY** position! Why were Arsenal bringing in another number 9 – and a world-class one too – when they had only just signed me a few months earlier? **MAYBE THEY DIDN'T BELIEVE IN ME AFTER ALL . . .**

When the next season began, I spent the first few games sitting on the bench, getting more and more frustrated. Why had I been dropped from the team? **It didn't seem fair.** What had I done wrong? It wasn't like I was playing badly. When I got the chance to come on, I usually scored, but apparently I still wasn't good enough to start. What was I going to do? There was only one answer in the end: **ADAPT.**

One day, the Arsenal manager, Pedro Martínez Losa, came to me with a crazy new idea: 'I think you'd make a great winger.'

A winger – really? But I'd played as a number 9 all my football career, since I was six years old! At first, I wasn't a fan of that plan at all, but if it meant I got more chances to play, then I was willing to give it a go. **WHO KNEW, MAYBE I WOULD LOVE IT AND BECOME THE NEXT DAVID BECKHAM?**

THE TWO NUMBER SEVENS

It's funny, as a young girl, I used to love watching **David Beckham** play on the wing for Manchester United and England, even though I was a striker at the time. Wearing the number 7 on his back, Beckham would whip in lots of incredible crosses, and now, years later, I wear the same shirt and I play the same position! I'd like to think I'm quite well known in the women's game for my crossing ability now, and that all started with watching him and wanting to do what he did. So thanks, Becks!

Moving from the middle of the pitch to out wide might not sound like a massive change, but trust me – it is. **As a winger, everything is totally different**: the way you defend, the way you attack, how you receive the ball, how you run with it . . .

So I had lots of work to do to add these powers to my skillset. First, I spent time studying top footballers who played in my new position to try to get a better understanding of what to do. Mo Salah was flying at Liverpool, so I watched him carefully, looking at the way he moved the ball, how he cut inside on to his stronger foot. Then, as soon as I saw something new that I could use/copy, I went out and practised on the training pitch, over and over again.

GET READY TO ROAR ACTIVITY

From the earlier activities in this chapter, you should now have a list of your teammates, opponents and role models that you think have superstar skills you can learn from. Now write down three parts of your sporting skillset that you'd like to work on and see if there is one of your heroes who does this brilliantly. Here's an example for you:

SKILL

HERO

Dedication

Kim Little

Cutting inside on to my stronger foot

Mo Salah

Crossing the ball

David Beckham

If you're struggling for ideas, my advice would be: **START WITH THE SMALL THINGS** – because so often they're the most important. Growing up, I remember a coach telling me, 'Every chance you get, go and kick a ball against a wall – left foot, right foot, again and again.'

SOUNDS SIMPLE, RIGHT? But it worked for me. I spent hours doing it, driving Mum and Dad mad with the noise, until it started to feel normal and natural for me to use both feet. These days, my right foot is still stronger, but I like to think my left is pretty lethal too! **It's truly one of my super-strengths.**

This doesn't just work for sport either – it works for anything you want to get good at! For example, if you have been selected to act in the school play, you could:

1. Write down all your favourite actors and the people you know who can act brilliantly

2. Identify areas you need to improve on

3. Study those actors and see what it is that makes them great. Borrow some of their style, mirror their confidence, act like a star – and then practise until you're on top of your game!

As I adapted to my new role as a winger, I didn't just throw out my old knowledge and skills. **No, I was adding to my skillset**, not taking anything away. **I WAS GROWING MY GAME, RAISING IT TO AN EVEN HIGHER LEVEL.** Plus, my previous experience actually gave me an advantage: I knew what a number 9 wanted from a winger because I had been a number 9 myself for years.

In the end, it all worked out and after a few months, Viv and I were linking up really well for Arsenal. I was adding more assists to my game, while still scoring lots of goals. Boom, I was becoming a better player, and we were becoming a **better team**!

That season, we went all the way and won the WSL title for the first time in seven years. After a long, hard season of lots of ups and a few downs, we finished on a big high, beating our main rivals Manchester City 1–0. We had done it; we were the English champions! What an emotional day that was – the relief of finally achieving our goal, mixed with the pure joy of **winning my first major team trophy**.

BASICALLY, THE BEST FEELING IN THE WORLD!

I'm not saying that changing my position changed everything for me, but it definitely had a big impact. I also got my first senior England call-up as a winger, and that's where I played at the Euros too. So yes, it's a role that I love now – **my Arsenal manager was right, after all**!

If you're ever asked to try something different in your sport – a new position, maybe, or a new technique – don't see it as a bad thing, like I did at first. It's the same with anything new in life. **Say yes**, **adapt** and **see it as a chance to learn and improve**, to add to your skillset. Because remember what I said at the beginning of this chapter:

YOU'VE GOT TO KEEP RAISING YOUR GAME!

BETH'S TOP THREE TOUGHEST OPPONENTS:

1
LUCY BRONZE, BARCELONA AND ENGLAND

2
ONA BATLLE, MANCHESTER UNITED AND SPAIN

3
GIULIA GWINN, BAYERN MUNICH AND GERMANY

Although we play together for our country, we've played against each other lots of times for our clubs, so I know how annoying she can be! Just when you think you've got past her, suddenly she's there again!

Quick, skilful and hard to beat

A really tough full-back to play against

BETH'S PRE-CHAPTER WARM-UP: THE OBJECT OBSTACLE COURSE

In life, we all have challenges to overcome, so let's try and make things fun by doing . . . an object obstacle course! It's good for:

- ✓ Co-ordination
- ✓ Concentration
- ✓ Speed
- ✓ Agility

WHAT TO DO: Collect up between five and ten SOFT objects, such as pillows, jumpers, socks and teddy bears. Place them in different spots around the space you're in.

YOUR CHALLENGE: GO! Weave your way through the object obstacle course as quickly as you can.

EXTRA TIME: Instead of running around the objects, why not try jumping over them?

TWIST IT UP: Fancy having a go at a game I like to call 'One, Two, Pea'? Sitting down at a table, each player will need three dried peas and a straw. The aim of the game is to use your straw to blow the peas off the table, one by one. The last pea is the winner!

CHAPTER SEVEN

LET DISAPPOINTMENTS DRIVE YOU ON

No matter how much you keep raising your game on and off the pitch, **no one is perfect**. Throughout life, you're going to have loads of success and achieve great things, but remember, there will always be things that go wrong along the way, and that's OK. **Injuries, disappointments, failures, frustrations – setbacks are a big part of sport and they're a big part of life too.**

Remember back in chapter three when I told you about my struggles with maths at school? Despite my best efforts, I wasn't getting the grades I wanted, and I would get so upset about that.

The earliest sporting setback I can remember came when I was eleven years old, playing in an all-day tournament for California girls. We were one of the best football teams in the area and we flew through to the semi-finals. But that's when **DISASTER STRUCK** for me. I was our star player and full of confidence, so when the ball ran loose, I raced in to try and win it back.

As I'm sure you know by now, **I'm a very competitive person**. I don't like to lose, whether it's a tackle or a match, so in I went, full commitment, zero fear. It was a fair, 50-50 challenge, but I must have slightly caught the girl because she got really upset. I tried saying sorry, even though I'd done nothing wrong, but the referee saw things differently. It turned out that he was a family member of one of our opponents, and he decided to send me off.

WHAT? NO WAY! It wasn't a yellow card, let alone a red one. I couldn't believe it. As I walked off the pitch, I felt distraught, like I'd let my whole team down. Fortunately, they managed to win the match without me, but my red card meant that I couldn't play in the final either. Instead, I had to sit and watch from the sidelines as we lost. **I was devastated.**

GET READY TO ROAR ACTIVITY

Can you think of any setbacks you've experienced or events that didn't go as you had hoped? These might be in sport or in school. If so, write them down on a piece of paper. Keep the piece of paper safe, as it's going to come in useful later!

As you can tell, I still remember that red card moment, but in this chapter we're not going to dwell on the negatives. Instead, we're going to focus on the positives and what it takes to come **bouncing back** from setbacks.

Although I was absolutely gutted at the time, I didn't let it get me down for long. Soon, I got back up and out on the football pitch, feeling more determined than ever. I wanted to make up for being sent off by helping my team to win the next tournament we played. **And guess what? We did!**

There were plenty more setbacks to come after that first red card, but to get to the big ones, I'm going to fast-forward to 2019. That summer, I had the honour of playing for England in my first-ever World Cup in France. Wow, what a proud feeling that was! I enjoyed so much of that tournament – my World Cup debut against Scotland, my assist for **Lucy Bronze** against Norway – **I WAS FLYING HIGH!** But ultimately, it all ended in bitter disappointment.

In the semi-finals, we faced the USA, the reigning champions and the team ranked number one in the world. We weren't afraid of them, though; no, we believed that if we played at our best, we could beat anyone, even the USA. Even when we went 1–0 down after only ten minutes, we kept believing. Nine minutes later, I got the ball on the left wing, looked up and crossed the ball into the box for **Ellen White** to finish. 1–1 – **hurray, we were back in the game**!

In that moment, what we needed was calm and concentration. But instead we got over-excited. We conceded another goal before half-time.

> # NOOOOOOOO!
> # IT WAS SO FRUSTRATING.

We didn't give up, though. We came back out and dominated the second half, and in the eighty-fourth minute, we won a penalty. But our captain, **Steph Houghton**, didn't catch the ball right and her shot was saved.

> # NOOOOOOOO,
> # AGAIN!

Soon, it was all over and England were out of the World Cup. It was heartbreaking to lose in a semi-final like that, when we knew we deserved better. Watching the final a few days later was hard because we felt that it could, and maybe should, have been us out there.

When you go through a big disappointment, it can be tempting to give up, but don't. **YOU'VE GOT TO KEEP GOING!** And to do that, you'll need to be resilient. You've probably heard that word before, but let me explain what it means:

If you're resilient, you recover quickly after something bad or difficult happens to you.

YOU DON'T LET IT GET YOU DOWN.

YOU DON'T BEAT YOURSELF UP ABOUT WHAT WENT WRONG.

INSTEAD, YOU COME BACK STRONGER.

Just like in everyday life, the world of sport is full of **highs and lows, wins and losses, ups and downs**, so it can teach you a lot about resilience. That World Cup was my first time playing in a major tournament and my first experience of dealing with that level of disappointment. I did find it difficult to move on, **but I bounced back stronger in the end**.

How? By doing four simple things:

MY FOUR GOLDEN RULES FOR ROARING BACK

1) TAKE SOME TIME TO SWITCH OFF

After something disappointing happens, it can be hard to motivate yourself again, which is why it's important to take some time to switch off, relax and recover. Don't stress yourself out over your setback. Instead, use it as an opportunity to take a break so you can come back energised. When I experience setbacks, I often want to escape and forget about football for a bit, but how? By cheering myself up and doing things I enjoy!

BETH'S TOP THREE WAYS TO FEEL BETTER ABOUT HERSELF:

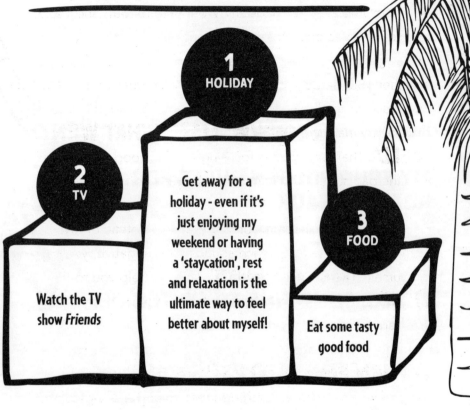

1 HOLIDAY

Get away for a holiday - even if it's just enjoying my weekend or having a 'staycation', rest and relaxation is the ultimate way to feel better about myself!

2 TV

Watch the TV show *Friends*

3 FOOD

Eat some tasty good food

But what about **YOU**? What would you choose to do to take your mind off your disappointment?

2) FOCUS ON THE POSITIVES

The next thing I do is try to think positively, instead of dwelling on what went wrong or punishing myself over the mistakes I made.

OK, so our semi-final had been a disappointing moment, but there were still parts of the tournament that I could be proud of. For example, I had made my World Cup debut, and I had also set up three goals for my teammates!

Whether your setback comes in sport or another part of life, give positive thinking a go. The next time you experience a setback, try making a **'WWW' LIST: 'WHAT WENT WELL'**. That way, you're focusing on the good stuff rather than the bad stuff, which can really help with worry and anxiety.

You can also start using the word **'YET'**. So instead of saying, 'I haven't won a medal', which sounds a bit negative, you say to yourself, **'I haven't won a medal YET'**. This can help you to think more positively. Sometimes things just take time, but you will get there eventually.

3) TURN PAIN INTO PROGRESS

Next, rather than staying sad for ages, whenever things don't go my way, I try to learn from what went wrong so I can do better next time. With my World Cup experience, I tried to think about how I could become a better player and be more successful next time. For example, I wanted to score at least one goal – hopefully, lots more – and perform better in the biggest moments. The more I thought about what I was going to do in the future, the more determined and focused I felt.

Underneath your 'WWW' list, add a second **'EBI' LIST:** **'EVEN BETTER IF'**. Write down things that you want to improve on for next time.

4) TRANSFORM FRUSTRATION INTO FUEL!

Finally, when you experience a setback, it's important to remind yourself why you love doing what you do and to channel all your energy into doing better next time – **turning that frustration into fuel!**

Sport can be a brilliant way to burn off all that stress and emotion. That's what I was going to do: let go of all my anger and swap it for drive and determination instead. I was going to channel my pain into playing even better football. Yes, I was going to come back better and stronger than ever, and prove my doubters wrong. **ROAAAAAAR!**

By the time I returned for pre-season at Arsenal, I was eager to play again. I was ready to keep going, fuelled by my disappointment, towards more major tournaments and more chances to win trophies. Early in our first WSL match against West Ham, I got the ball on the edge of the box and **BANG!** **. . . GOAL!**

I WAS BACK!

GET READY TO ROAR ACTIVITY

Next to each of the setbacks you noted down on your piece of paper in the last activity, now write down:

1. What you could have done to switch off and cheer yourself up

2. What went well – **think positively**! Was it as bad as it seemed or were there things that still made you proud?

3. What would have been even better if . . . Now think about what you could improve for next time

4. Why you want to do better next time – what is it that drives you on and makes you want to succeed? What fuels you to keep trying?

NOW, GO GET 'EM!

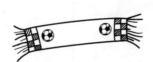

I didn't know it then, as I celebrated that goal with my Arsenal teammates, but there were much bigger setbacks ahead.

10 May 2021. I remember the exact date because it was the day after my birthday. With the Tokyo Olympics coming up in July, the manager of the Team GB women's football team, **Hege Riise**, was about to announce her final squad, and I was really hoping to be selected. I thought I had been doing everything right: working hard, keeping fit, training well, playing well and getting goals and assists for Arsenal. **As I've said earlier in this book, I love the Olympics, and I was desperate to be a part of it.**

That morning, my Arsenal teammate Jordan Nobbs rang me up to say that she'd just received the nightmare phone call: she hadn't made the squad. **NOOOOOO!**

I was gutted for Jordan, and I was suddenly worried about my own chances too. **Was I going to get the same horrible call?** I spent the rest of the day in a state of dread, waiting and willing the phone not to ring. But at 4.30 in the afternoon, it did. My heart sank straight away. **It was bad news**: two years after playing for England at the 2019 World Cup, I had been left out of the Team GB squad.

Missing out on the Olympics was a massive setback for me. I couldn't understand it, and at first, **I just felt angry**. Angry at myself, angry at everyone, really. Luckily, I had Jordan, who was in the same sad situation as me, so we spent the whole summer together, moaning to each other and . . . **it was time to bring in my four golden rules for roaring back again**. So I:

1) SWITCHED OFF

Jordan and I still had a big sporting summer, but as spectators rather than players.

WIMBLEDON

I've always loved watching tennis on TV, and especially Wimbledon, but I'd never been able to go and watch it live before. Luckily, one of the British women's players, Harriet Dart, is a big Arsenal fan, and she invited us to come and watch her play in the doubles tournament. **It was amazing to be there and to enjoy a sunny day with lots of strawberries and cream!**

UEFA EURO 2020

That summer, the men's Euros were also taking place, and a lot of the matches were played at Wembley. We managed to get tickets for the semi-final and final, which turned out to be very different experiences. The final against Italy was scary because of all the crowd trouble, but the semi-final against Denmark was a fun game to watch. **The atmosphere was unbelievable** and it was so brilliant to see the team playing so well together. At that time, I wasn't really looking as far ahead as the women's Euros in 2022, but later on, **I definitely did use those nights as inspiration**.

Despite all that sporting fun we had, **my Olympic disappointment didn't go away**. I still wished that I was there. While the tournament was taking place in Tokyo, I was doing pre-season training at Arsenal. I remember running angrily up and down the pitch during a fitness test, thinking, **'WHY AM I DOING THIS? WHY AM I HERE? I COULD BE AT THE OLYMPICS – I SHOULD BE AT THE OLYMPICS!'**

At that moment, I had so much rage inside of me, partly because of football, but mostly because of family. Earlier that week, I had found out some awful news about Mum: she had been diagnosed with cancer. I was devastated. I hoped that playing football and seeing friends would help take my mind off things, and they did a bit, but not enough. Life just felt so unfair, like my world was being turned upside down.

Suddenly, I stopped running and just stood there for a minute, taking long, deep breaths. Something had clicked in my mind; **I couldn't carry on that way**. It was time to . . .

2) TURN NEGATIVES INTO POSITIVES

Sometimes, the setbacks you experience will be beyond your control and no one's fault. When that happens, all you can do is try to accept and move forward. I thought to myself:

> **'Why are you so angry about something that you can't change? Just go out there and enjoy each moment.'**

Life's too short for holding grudges. They can really weigh you down, and it's just not worth it. Why waste energy on negative feelings when you could be using it for positives?

To bounce back from my disappointments, **I needed to stop dwelling on the past** – the stuff that had already happened and I couldn't change – and start focusing on the future – the stuff that I could change and do something about. I had to think more positively and treat each and every day as a chance to progress and improve, as a person and a player.

Right then, on that training pitch, the feelings inside of me shifted. **I was going to bounce back just like I had in the past, by . . .**

3) TURNING PAIN INTO PROGRESS

The awful news about Mum was a massive wake-up call for me. I had to start **making the most of every day I had**. I was going to use my frustrations – at football and at life – to push me forward and to help me grow as a player and a person. Suddenly, I felt more **determined** and **focused** than ever. I was ready to . . .

4) TRANSFORM FRUSTRATION INTO FUEL!

I had to get back to enjoying my football again. Otherwise, what was the point? I had lost a bit of my love for the game, and I needed to find it again. To do that, I had to go back, back to the beginning, back to being that happy six-year-old girl running around a pitch with a ball at my feet.

If you have setbacks on your journey, **always remember the reasons why you started doing what you're doing**, the reasons we wrote down back in chapter three. For me with football, they were **FREEDOM, FUN, GOALS** and **FRIENDSHIPS**. I'm sure yours will be different for your particular passion, but whatever they are, don't ever forget them!

Sadly, that Olympic summer wasn't the end of my setbacks. In November 2022, just months after the Euros, I suffered the most serious injury of my career. **I tore my ACL**, one of the key ligaments in the knee, which meant I faced a long time away from the football pitch and a real challenge to get fit again.

When I found out the news, I was devastated, of course, but I didn't give up. I knew what I needed to do and the resilience I needed to show. I had overcome disappointments and heartbreak before, so I knew that I could, and would, bounce back again. No matter how long it would take, and even if I missed the 2023 World Cup, there would be plenty more major games and tournaments to come.

Plus, I was able to find one very important positive amongst all the pain. Mum's cancer was sadly getting worse, but because I was out injured, **I was able to sit, reflect and spend more precious time with her**.

So if you suffer a setback, don't give up and don't despair. Instead, stay strong and resilient, don't ever give up on your dreams and . . .

LET YOUR DISAPPOINTMENTS DRIVE YOU ON.

HERO: JESSICA ENNIS-HILL

As someone who plays as part of a team, I admire anyone who does an individual sport. **Tennis players, gymnasts, athletes** – you have my **total respect**! Why? Because in bad moments, I have my teammates there to pick me up and help me bounce back, but in an individual sport, it's just you out there on your own, making all the decisions and

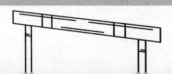
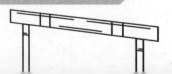

motivating yourself. Everything is on you, and you've got to have amazing mental strength to deal with that.

That mindset is one of the many reasons why I think **Jessica Ennis-Hill** is so incredible. Another is her sport, the heptathlon. I played lots of different sports and then chose to focus on one: football. But to do the heptathlon at the Olympic Games, you have to be at the highest, world-class level in **SEVEN** different sporting events! The 100m hurdles, the 200m, the 800m, the high jump, the shot put, the long jump and the javelin throw – wow, that's **A LOT** of talent for one person to have, isn't it? And if one of those events doesn't go so well, you have to pick yourself up and move straight on to the next.

Jessica's story has always inspired me too. As a young athlete, she had setbacks and missed the 2008 Olympics due to injury, but she didn't let it get her down. Instead, she worked hard on her recovery, and the next year, she came back to win the first of her three World Championships. I always loved watching her in action, and seeing her win Olympic Gold in 2012 was one of my all-time favourite sporting moments. Then, in 2016, she competed at the Olympics in Rio, and she won the silver medal.

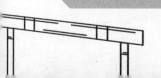
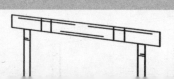

BETH'S PRE-CHAPTER WARM-UP: THE BEANBAG BALANCE

Got your head in the game now? Good, because for this chapter, we're kicking off with a . . . beanbag balance! It's good for:

- ✓ Co-ordination
- ✓ Being slow and steady
- ✓ Standing tall

WHAT TO DO: Grab a beanbag and place it on top of your head, where it's not going to fall off straight away.

YOUR CHALLENGE: Walk as far as you can with the beanbag still balanced on your head. If it falls, start again!

EXTRA TIME: If that's too easy, try doing something more energetic with that beanbag on your head, like skipping, dancing or running!

TWIST IT UP: Grab a small ball, place it on top of your head and see how long you can keep it balanced there.

CHAPTER EIGHT

FLICK THAT SUPERSTAR SWITCH

Are you feeling strong and determined now, ready to overcome any challenges that life throws at you? I hope so, because in this next chapter, we're going to be raising our game to the highest level. It's time for you to flick the switch and go from star to **SUPERSTAR!**

'OK great, but what actually makes someone a superstar?' – you might be wondering.

IF SO, GOOD QUESTION!

In 2022, I played the best football I've ever played in my career, taking my game to a world-class level. Since the Euros, lots of people have asked me **'Why?'** and **'How?'** that happened, so let me try to explain by breaking things down into two halves, just like a game of football:

FIRST HALF: THE SUPERSTAR SKILLSET – WHAT MAKES YOU REALLY GOOD AT YOUR SPORT?

We can't all be **mind-blowingly amazing** at everything in life or at every part of the sport we love. For example, I'm rubbish at singing and I don't care! **It's just not my thing.** I also like to think I'm pretty good at heading, but I'm not the tallest player around and I don't score that many headed goals. It's something that I keep practising, but I'm never going to be the best in the world at heading, and that's OK.

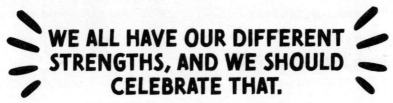

WE ALL HAVE OUR DIFFERENT STRENGTHS, AND WE SHOULD CELEBRATE THAT.

In chapter six, we talked about working on your weaknesses and adding exciting new powers to your skillset, but now we need to add the **X-factor**, and for this, I have a new hero for you to meet . . .

HERO: SARINA WIEGMAN

As you'll see throughout the next few chapters, my England manager has had a major influence on me, as a player and as a person. There are many, many things that I want to thank her for, but I'll start with this one. At one of our very first meetings after she took the job in September 2021, Sarina sat me down and told me the things that she thought I could improve on, the strengths that I could turn into **SUPER-strengths.**

Sorry, I can't tell you everything because that would be giving away my secrets – my winning superstar formula! – but here are a couple of the strengths we talked about that day:

MY FOOTBALL BRAIN: I've always been an intelligent player, but Sarina wanted me to use my quick football brain more in the biggest moments to help us win matches. Whether it was picking out a **killer pass** that could split open a defence or delivering a cross into a dangerous area, she believed that I was smart enough and capable enough to change games in an instant.

MY SHOOTING: Scoring goals has always been one of my strengths as a footballer, ever since I was six years old. My record for England was good, but Sarina believed it could be a lot better. She wanted me to attack with confidence and make sure I was always in the right area. 'Don't be afraid to make mistakes,' she told me. 'You're a forward – sometimes you'll miss and sometimes you'll score, but just make sure you're in the box when that ball comes in.'

YES, BOSS!

Now that Sarina had picked out my **key strengths**, it was down to me. I had lots of hard work to do, to turn them into **SUPER-strengths**.

In every football match I played, I tried to be brave and find clever ways to change the game. I practised making perfectly timed runs into the six-yard box, staying alert to every opportunity and scoring as many goals as possible. And so, step by step, day by day, those strengths turned into my **SUPER-strengths**.

TA-DA!

126

And it doesn't just work for sport – you can apply this to **ANYTHING** you want to be good at.

GET READY TO ROAR ACTIVITY

What makes you really good at the thing you love or the sport you play? Make a list of what you see as your three **greatest strengths**. Or if you need some help choosing, why not ask one of your champions from chapter four, the people who make you feel safe and supported and will always have your back. What do they think you're best at?

Once you've got your list of top strengths, how are you going to turn them into **SUPER-STRENGTHS**? Next to each strength, have a go at writing down something you could do to improve in that area. Maybe you need to do a particular kind of practice, or maybe you just need to be braver and use that strength more in the big moments.

OK, first half over. Moving on to the . . .

SECOND HALF: THE SUPERSTAR MINDSET – HOW CAN YOU MAKE THE MOST OF YOUR SUPER-STRENGTHS?

Having super-strengths is great, but you've also got to know how to use them when you need them most. When the pressure's on, how are you going to make the most of your talent and flick that **superstar switch**?

In chapters six and seven, we talked about hard work, dedication, perseverance and resilience, which are all important parts of the superstar mindset. But now, we need to add the **X-factor**, by . . .

Working out when you perform at your best:

Is it when you're angry?

When you're happy?

When you're calm?

When you're excited?

When you're pumped up or chilled out?

Think back to your best-ever match, competition or tournament: **can you remember how you were feeling that day?**

Then think back to moments where things didn't go so well for you: did you feel like **there was something missing in those moments? Were your emotions different on those days?**

I'll give you some time to think, because I'm guessing you probably haven't asked yourself that question before. I definitely didn't, but now, when I think back to the best goals I scored when I was starting out, I know what my answer to the first question would be:

I did my best when I was feeling happy, calm and free

and

when I was just me being me.

And twenty years later, the answer is still exactly the same. After that day at Arsenal pre-season training when I stopped **worrying** and **overthinking** things and just tried to enjoy every moment, what happened next?

AMAZING THINGS, OF COURSE!

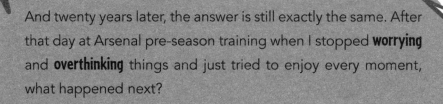

GET READY TO ROAR ACTIVITY

Your superstar switch is a personal thing and it's something that you learn from experience, as you go through good and bad moments. It's about what works, what doesn't and what helps get the best out of **YOU** – not just in sport, but in all areas of life. What makes you **shine the brightest** at school, at home and when you're out playing with your friends?

As you search for that superstar switch, here are two fun activities to try:

1) Imagine you're an action figure or superhero. If you like drawing, you could design your outfit – and why not give yourself a fun catchphrase too?

Personally, I'd go for **'ROOOOOAAAAAAAAAR!'**

With one flick of a button, you come to life, going from normal you to . . . **SUPERSTAR YOU**! But tell me: what causes that switch to flick on?

2) If you like maths, try thinking of your superstar switch as a sum. So, for me, it might be something like:

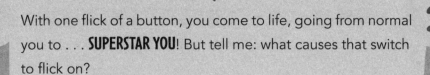

FREEDOM + FUN – WORRY = TING! FLASH! SUPERSTAR!

That's **MY** winning formula, for football and for life. When I feel free, have fun and stop worrying, I become a better player, as well as a better friend and a happier person.

Now it's your turn!

By the time the 2021–22 WSL season kicked off, I had started falling in love with football again. I felt less angry and more determined, and my new Arsenal manager, **Jonas Eidevall**, was encouraging me to attack with energy and freedom, and to just be who I wanted to be.

YES, BOSS! But before we move on, there's one more bit I need to add to my superstar sum:

FREEDOM + FUN + **COMPETITION** – WORRY = TING! FLASH! SUPERSTAR!

You see, that summer, Arsenal had signed two new experienced, international forwards: **Tobin Heath** and **Nikita Parris**. Suddenly, my place in the starting line-up wasn't so secure any more; **I had work to do**.

For some people, that sense of competition can feel very stressful, but for me, it's actually a good thing. When the level rises around me, it **pushes me out of my comfort zone and makes me perform better**. I was determined to stay in the Arsenal team, so I fought even harder to be the best I could be.

In our first game of the season, we faced our big London rivals, Chelsea, at the Emirates Stadium. The match was tied 1–1 at half-time, but early in the second half, everything changed.

ZOOM! As I chased after Vivianne Miedema's through-ball, I was determined to get there first before the Chelsea defenders, and I did. Then I dribbled forward with the ball, feeling like I was a little kid again. In that moment, it didn't really matter that we were playing a big game at the Emirates; I could have been anywhere, even back at the local playing field in Hinderwell. I was just having fun on a football pitch. When I reached the edge of the box, I slowed down, shifted the ball on to my left foot and

BANG! . . . GOAL!

As I threw my arms out wide and let out a **loud roar**, I felt so alive and free. **I FELT UNSTOPPABLE.** Ten minutes later, I raced into the Chelsea box again, dribbled around the goalkeeper and calmly slid the ball into the net. 3–1 to Arsenal!

TING! FLASH! I had successfully flicked that superstar switch.

Finding your superstar switch is the first step; the next is working out **how to keep flicking that switch on, again and again**, even when you don't feel at your best. On days when I'm not as happy, calm and free as I'd like to be, I use feel-good music to get myself into the zone. Luckily, for both Arsenal and England, I have 'Team DJ' **Leah Williamson** by my side, selecting the right tunes!

What could you do to help get you in the mood to perform at your best?

With England, our manager Sarina gave me even more freedom. She had her principles and how she wanted us to play as a team, but she was always encouraging us to express ourselves on the pitch — so I was ready to flick the switch and put my new **SUPER**-strengths into practice.

I scored one goal in Sarina's first match, as we beat Macedonia **8-0**,

I set up four more for my teammates as we scored **10** against Luxembourg,

and then in the third match against Northern Ireland, I came on in the sixty-third minute and still found time to score my **first international hat-trick**.

TING! FLASH! GOALS! ASSISTS! GAME-CHANGING MOMENTS!

I was on fire for England, as well as for Arsenal. I was having fun and playing with freedom. It felt like a weight had been lifted off my shoulders and my parents could see the difference

too. 'It's nice to see you playing like a little kid again!' Dad said to me.

The search for your superstar switch may take some time, but trust me, it'll be worth it in the end. **BECAUSE ONCE YOU FIND IT, YOU'RE GOING TO FEEL UNSTOPPABLE!**

Once you've flicked the switch to unlock your superstar skills, **what are you waiting for**? It's time to take your talent all the way to the top.

Hero: VIVIANNE MIEDEMA

Thierry Henry and Dennis Bergkamp, Woody and Buzz Lightyear from *Toy Story* – **all the best partnerships know how to get the best out of each other.**

That's definitely true with me and Viv too. I've been lucky enough to play with her for a long time now, since she first joined Arsenal in 2017, and she played a massive part in spurring me on to flick that superstar switch.

I mean, how could I not learn something from a striker who scored 100 goals in her first 110 games for the club? She's already the all-time record goal scorer in the WSL, as well as in the history of the Dutch national team. In other words, she's an **ABSOLUTE SUPERSTAR**! Every day I was seeing Viv up close, performing at a world-class level – **the goals, the touch, the skill, the focus, the consistency** – and that inspired me to think, 'OK, maybe I could do the same.'

When she's out on the football pitch, Viv can sometimes look so chilled that it seems like she doesn't really care, but that's not true at all. In fact, it's completely the opposite – but to perform at her best, she goes into her **ice-cold zone**. That's her superstar switch. A-ha – see, I was learning! During the 2021–22 WSL season, we took our double act to the next level. On the pitch, we pushed each other hard but we also had lots of fun together, teaming up for 25 goals and 16 assists. And off the pitch, we also started dating.

Viv's a very calm character, and she's helped me lots, especially in dealing with the extra attention and expectations. She's been in the same position herself and understands how heavy the pressure can feel sometimes. She's been seen as a superstar since she was fifteen years old, so she's able to say to me, 'This worked for me . . .' or 'I did this but it didn't go so well . . .' After helping me reach that **world-class level**, now she's helping me to stay there.

BETH'S TOP THREE GREATEST GOALS:

2
VS BRIGHTON

1
VS SWEDEN

3
VS BRAZIL

To help Arsenal
win the WSL title,
28 April 2019

Euro semi-finals,
26 July 2022

SheBelieves
Cup, 27
February 2019

BETH'S PRE-CHAPTER WARM-UP: THE WARRIOR POSE

This chapter is all about feeling confident and fearless, but sadly yoga doesn't have a lioness pose yet, so instead we'll go for the . . . warrior pose! It's good for:

- ✓ Making you happy
- ✓ Making you calm
- ✓ Boosting confidence
- ✓ Concentration
- ✓ Releasing nerves

WHAT TO DO: Stand up tall with your feet wide apart. Turn your right toes out and press your left heel away. Bend your right knee deeply and stretch your arms out at shoulder height. While holding the pose, take lots of deep breaths to **relax your body and calm your mind.**

CHAPTER NINE

BELIEVE IN YOURSELF (LIKE OTHERS BELIEVE IN YOU)

YOU CAN DO THIS; I BELIEVE IN YOU, SO NOW I NEED YOU TO BELIEVE IN YOURSELF.

Self-belief is such an important part of any success. I don't mean arrogance and acting like you're better than everyone else. I mean having **confidence in your own abilities and the belief that you can do whatever you put your mind to**. Going into the Euros, I really believed in myself and my ability. As you'll soon discover, that is the key to unlocking your dreams too.

It took me a long time to find my inner confidence. As we explored back in chapter four, my mum and dad always believed in my football talent, long before I believed in myself. But your family is your family, right? **They're supposed to say nice things about you!** Often, those words don't have the same impact coming from your own parents as they do when they come from your friends, your teachers, your teammates and your coaches. When those people tell you they believe in you, it can make a massive difference.

At that early meeting with Sarina where we talked about my 'super-strengths', she used a **very powerful phrase** to describe the potential that she believed I had:

'WITH A BIT OF WORK, YOU COULD BE WORLD CLASS.'

'WORLD CLASS'? I had never even thought about using that phrase to describe myself, not until Sarina said it out loud that day. But just hearing her say those words gave me so much confidence, and I left the room with a spring in my step, thinking, **'Yeah! Maybe I could be world class . . .'**

But despite me playing well for Arsenal and at all the England training camps, I still had work to do if I wanted to secure a spot in the Euros starting line-up. Even when I scored four goals against North Macedonia, Sarina carried on swapping her wingers around: me, **Chloe Kelly, Nikita Parris, Fran Kirby, Lauren Hemp** . . .

I was even beginning to wonder if maybe Sarina had changed her mind about me and my world-class potential, when one day she turned to me and said, 'I'm just not sure which wing you're better on, Beth: right or left.'

REALLY? I felt like I was playing well on the right for Arsenal, but perhaps I wasn't doing enough to impress my manager.

When you get disappointing feedback, **it's easy to take it badly and let it knock your confidence. BUT SARINA'S MESSAGE WASN'T NEGATIVE; IT WAS POSITIVE**. She was challenging me, giving me the extra push that I needed to step up, be better and prove myself. Instead of feeling down and letting doubts creep in, I had to stay positive and start standing out above the rest in my preferred position. Sarina had showed that she believed I had the potential to keep growing and improving and become 'world class', but now, to reach that level, **I HAD TO BELIEVE IN MYSELF**.

The next England camp was the last one before the Euros. I knew that if I was going to secure my spot on the right wing, it was now or never. I started the first match against Belgium, but Sarina took me off at half-time. Then in the second against the Netherlands, Chloe started on the wing and I came on at half-time.

Right, this was it; my second chance to shine. I could do this . . .

Early in the second half, as Lauren looked up to cross the ball in from the left, I raced forward and slid in at the back post, determined to score . . . **GOAL!**

'COME ONNNN!' I roared, giving Lauren a big hug, and in the last minute of the match, I kept calm, kept believing and scored again.

Two goals from the right wing – it was me saying, 'Look, Sarina, this is what I can bring to the team!' **The timing was perfect.** It felt like a massive moment, a huge turning point in my England career and for me as a person. It was a huge boost for my self-belief; **I was ready to become a world-class superstar . . .**

GET READY TO ROAR ACTIVITY

Are there any positive words or phrases that you could use to help give you a confidence boost at the crucial moment? If so, write them down on a piece of paper.

It could be some good advice you've seen somewhere or heard from someone. As a kid, I was always one of the smallest players on the pitch, so to stop me from feeling scared, Dad used to say to me, **'They bigger they are, the harder they fall.'** That phrase stuck with me, and it helped me to stay fearless out on the football pitch.

Or it could be a motivational message from you to yourself, like:

ALL YOU CAN DO IS YOUR BEST

YOU ARE AMAZING

YOU CAN DO THIS

If you then say it out loud to yourself, that's called **POSITIVE SELF-TALK** and it can be a powerful tool in high-pressure moments. **Give it a go!**

Personally, I don't really talk to myself when I'm out on the pitch, but if I need some extra motivation in the middle of a match, I have an action I do instead: I sort my socks out and pull them up. It's like a reset to go again.

Is there any action you could do to boost your self-belief?

GET READY TO ROAR ACTIVITY

Another great tool some people use to build up their self-belief is something called **VISUALISATION**. Visualisation is when you picture yourself performing a task, so that when you then do it for real, you feel more confident about it. Say you take free-kicks for your team. In the build-up to a big match, you could form a detailed mental image of you scoring a fantastic free-kick, including:

THE PITCH – muddy mess or slick surface?

YOUR RUN-UP – long or short?

THE WALL OF DEFENDERS IN FRONT OF YOU – big or small?

YOUR STRIKE – a curler into the top corner or a rocket, straight and low?

THE KEEPER – dives or doesn't even move because your strike is so good?

And of course:

THE CELEBRATION – knee-slide or leaping fist pump?

It's all about approaching the key moments with confidence in your own ability. In chapter seven, we talked about the power of positive thinking to help you bounce back from setbacks that have already happened, but positive thinking can also help you to mentally prepare for the next big challenge ahead. If you're getting ready to compete in a cup final, for example, visualising the winning moment as you lift the trophy can help to improve your performance and reduce your nerves.

This tool can help you in other parts of life too. Let's say you're feeling anxious about going to the school disco – well, visualise yourself going, having a great time, dancing with your friends and then going home happy. The more you imagine yourself doing something, the more you believe that you can do it. **GIVE IT A GO – GOOD LUCK!**

By the time the Euros began, I had built up so much self-confidence that I actually **felt pretty calm** about it. Yes, England were the tournament hosts and one of the favourites to win it, but what was the point in putting too much pressure on myself? It was my first-ever Euros and **I had nothing to lose**; I was just going to go out there and have fun on the football pitch, playing the sport I loved. **COULD I PERFORM AT A WORLD-CLASS LEVEL? YES, I COULD!**

FIRST UP: Austria, in the opening game of the tournament. It was an **emotional** and **nerve-wracking** experience for us, walking out in front of sixty-five thousand fans at Old Trafford, with all eyes on us and high expectations too. Could we stay calm and confident out there? **Yes and no . . .** With the pressure on, we definitely didn't perform at our best. That can happen sometimes in the biggest moments; it's only natural to feel a bit nervous. But in the end, we did get the win, and that was all that mattered.

Well, almost all that mattered, anyway. Because who scored the winning goal? **THAT'S RIGHT, ME!**

Even though the moment was over in a flash, it felt to me like it was all happening in slow motion:

Fran's long pass **floating through the air,**

my run in behind the Austria defence,

my first touch to control the ball and set myself up for the shot . . .

In that split second, I somehow still had time to think about my shooting options. **High or low? Left or right? Power or accuracy?**

The Austria keeper, **Manuela Zinsberger**, is my Arsenal teammate, so I know her strengths. She's excellent at saving low shots to her left and right, so I decided to lift the ball over her head instead.

But as soon as I kicked the ball, **I started panicking**. Oh no, had I made the wrong decision? Had I put enough power on it? As the ball bounced down, a defender chased after it and cleared it away, but I was pretty sure the ball had already gone over the line, and I was right. The signal on the referee's watch went off:

GOAL!

I threw my arms up, I punched the air with both fists and then I roared, with a mix of joy and relief. We were winning, and I was off the mark at the Euros already. As I'm sure you can imagine, scoring the winner at Old Trafford gave my self-belief a massive extra boost, especially

as someone who was a childhood Manchester United fan!

But while my **confidence was up**, I couldn't risk getting carried away. Self-belief doesn't mean blindly believing you will always win. **I NEEDED TO STAY FOCUSED AND DISCIPLINED.** After that win, we moved straight on to preparing for our next match against Norway. They're an amazing team with lots of quality players, but we knew that to finish top of our group, we were going to have to beat them. And we believed that we could beat them too.

The first ten minutes were tight and cagey, but then we got a penalty, which **Georgia Stanway** scored. After that, we settled down and found our rhythm, especially **Lucy Bronze** and I, who were linking up brilliantly on the right. **IT FELT AS IF WE COULD READ EACH OTHER'S MINDS:** what we were going to do next, where we were going to run. **Every chance we got, we raced forward together**, causing the Norway left-back all kinds of problems. With each attack, my belief in myself was growing. After a one-two with Lucy, I fired the ball across the six-yard box for Lauren to tap in. 2–0!

And amazingly, that was only just the beginning. By half-time it was 5–0, and I had grabbed two more goals of my own: a header (pretty rare for me!) and then a left-foot finish after dribbling through the Norway defence with some quick footwork. **HONESTLY, MY CONFIDENCE WAS SO HIGH THAT I FELT LIKE I COULD DO ANYTHING!**

I had to wait a while, but eventually I did get my third goal of the game. I was more determined than ever. In the eightieth minute, **Keira Walsh** had a shot saved by the keeper, but as the ball bounced down, I rushed in to reach it first and get the rebound. 8–0 – hurray,

HAT-TRICK!

WOW, WHAT A NIGHT! Sometimes, you just have those spells where everything you touch turns to gold. That Norway match was one of those for me – one of my all-time favourites for sure!

Now that the goals were flowing, they kept on coming. In our last group match against Northern Ireland, we won 5–0, and I scored the second, with some more quick footwork in the box.

Three games, three wins and, for me, five goals already. I was off to a fantastic start in the tournament and I was feeling great. I had

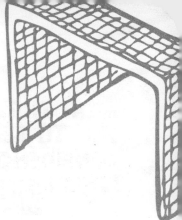

friends and old teammates texting me the whole time, saying, 'Woah, what have you been eating? You're on fire – you're finally showing what we've seen for a long time!'

After years of other people believing in me, **now, at last, I was also believing in myself,** and as a result, I was beginning to reach my potential. **AND THINGS WERE JUST ABOUT TO GET BIGGER AND BETTER . . .**

Back in chapter four, you wrote down a list of your champions, the people who believe in you, cheer for you and want you to achieve your dreams.

BUT NOW YOU HAVE TO BELIEVE IT TOO.

I get it, sometimes it's hard. I still find it difficult from time to time – in fact, you will be surprised how many professional footballers will have a wobble, even though they're at the top of their game! **THAT'S NORMAL. WE'RE ALL HUMAN.** Sometimes the doubts can come from comparing yourself to others and thinking that you'll never be as good as them. But as we discovered in chapter six, it's much better to learn from others. See what makes them awesome, and then apply it to your own life.

AT THE SAME TIME, YOU NEED TO BELIEVE THAT YOU ARE INCREDIBLE.

BECAUSE YOU ARE!

REMEMBER: I BELIEVE IN YOU, SO NOW I NEED YOU TO BELIEVE IN YOURSELF.

'OK, but where do I begin?' you might be wondering. Well, if I ever start to doubt myself, I try to do three simple things:

1) Remind myself of what I've already achieved in the past

If you've done something before, then you can do it again!

2) Keep performing well in the present

Because the more you succeed, the more confident you'll feel that you can keep on succeeding.

3) Think positively about the future

When you think positively, you become more confident. When you become more confident, you are more likely to **reach your goals.**

Hero: Lucy Bronze

Lucy and I have played together for England for a long time now, and during the 2022 Euros, we formed a formidable partnership on the right wing: her in defence and me in attack. Talk about a dream team, eh!

We're quite similar characters in many ways: most of the time we're pretty chilled off the football pitch, but once we're on it, we're on it! When we worked together, like we did in that game against Norway, we were **totally unstoppable.**

I trusted Lucy, and I knew that she trusted me too. But still, it's always nice to hear these things out loud, isn't it? During the Euros, we were all put into pairs for a team-bonding exercise, and my partner was Lucy. We had to do a series of tasks together, and at the end, there was a postbox where we could write messages to each other. Lucy's message to me that day is one that I'll never forget:

'I always knew you had this in you – you just needed to find it yourself.'

For someone of Lucy's experience and quality to say that about me, to show that she had always believed in me, felt absolutely amazing. It gave me a real confidence boost at just the right time.

BETH'S TOP THREE GREATEST GAMES:

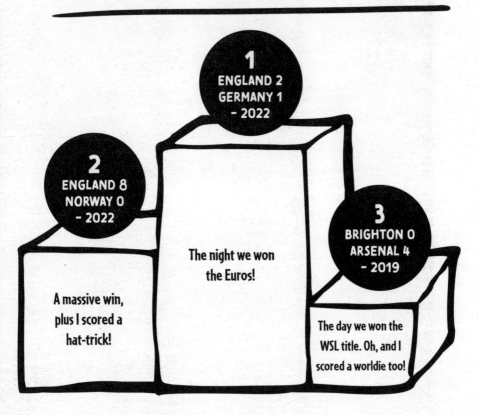

1
ENGLAND 2
GERMANY 1
– 2022

The night we won the Euros!

2
ENGLAND 8
NORWAY 0
– 2022

A massive win, plus I scored a hat-trick!

3
BRIGHTON 0
ARSENAL 4
– 2019

The day we won the WSL title. Oh, and I scored a worldie too!

BETH'S PRE-CHAPTER WARM-UP: THE TRUST TEST

This chapter is all about teamwork, so grab a friend and get ready for . . . the trust test! It's good for:

- ✓ Teamwork
- ✓ Concentration
- ✓ Communication
- ✓ Trust

WHAT TO DO: Person A puts on a blindfold (a scarf, sock or jumper will do), and person B places an object somewhere in the room. They must then lead person A to the object, using only words as directions. Person A has to trust person B to guide them correctly, so please, please make sure there are no dangerous obstacles in the way!

YOUR CHALLENGE: If using words seems too easy, try using signals instead. So for example, one hand clap might mean take a step forwards and two hand claps might mean take a step backwards. Just make sure you agree the signals before the blindfold goes on!

CHAPTER TEN

WORK TOGETHER, WIN TOGETHER

I was on fire at the Euros and full of belief, but I wasn't the only one. After three wins out of three in the group stage, all of us Lionesses were feeling great.

'TEAMWORK MAKES THE DREAM WORK'

– have you ever heard someone say that before? I'm guessing you have, but I want you to hear it again from me. **In life, we might think we have to do things by ourselves.** For example, you might think winning a race or passing an exam is down to you and you alone. But behind every success is a big team effort.

WORK TOGETHER, WIN TOGETHER – that's

what we Lionesses did at the Euros. We worked hard as a team and we won the tournament, **making our dreams come true**.

Teamwork is so important, whether you're playing a team sport like me or you're acting as an individual. I've already talked about the importance of champions and comfort blankets, but in this chapter we're going to focus on teammates and working together to win together.

By the time the Euros began, we Lionesses were feeling more united than ever because we had spent so much time together, on and off the football pitch. In the past, England managers had chopped and changed, picking lots of different players, but Sarina preferred to work with the **same smaller, tighter squad all the time**. That meant that we'd all been through the same journey and experienced everything together: **the big wins, the close wins and the hard-fought draws; the good days and the bad days**. We knew what each other had been through and how hard we'd all worked to prepare for this. We Lionesses were willing

to do anything for each other. **WHY?** Because we were more than just teammates; **we were friends**. Friendship makes a massive difference, especially in a team sport like football.

Playing sport is a brilliant way to make new friends, and it's also a great way to learn about **teamwork** and **collaboration**. As I've said throughout this book, we're all different, with different skills and different personalities, and if we bring all of our talents together, we can become bigger and better!

TOGETHERNESS was a real gamechanger for us at the Euros. It was our **X-factor**, our **superpower**, if you like. If I had to describe the special Lionesses spirit in three words, I'd go for:

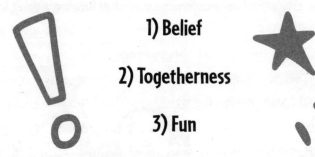

1) Belief

2) Togetherness

3) Fun

Those qualities are essential for a team on the sports field, but they're also essential for a cast of actors performing a play, or a group of students putting on a school assembly. So no matter what team you're in, here are **three tips** for making those around you **ROAR**!

1) SUPPORT EACH OTHER

Always stick together and look after each other, even when something goes wrong or someone makes a mistake. In fact, **ESPECIALLY** when that happens.

After topping our group, we faced Spain in the Euro quarter-finals. They're one of the **best teams in the world** when it comes to passing the ball around, and early in the second half, they broke through our defence and took the lead.

UH OH, we were losing for the first time all tournament. It was also the first goal we had conceded, so it was a disappointing moment for us. **What were we going to do now? How were we going to react?**

In previous tournaments when we went 1–0 down, our heads had dropped and we had failed to fight back. Sometimes, when the pressure's on, you can lose your composure, but Sarina brought that back – to me and to the whole squad. **THIS ENGLAND TEAM WAS BUILT DIFFERENTLY**; we weren't going to crumble under the pressure. We were united: **we believed in each other, we believed in Sarina and she believed in us**.

When something goes wrong, it's so easy to blame others,

but that's not going to get you anywhere. To get the best out of each other, you've got to make each other feel good, not bad. **You need to work as a team** to solve what's going wrong, and **the answer is rarely just one person**. So instead of moaning and blaming, **WE STOOD TALL AND TOGETHER**, with the same look of focus and determination on our faces that said,

'WE ARE NOT GIVING UP. WE ARE NOT GOING HOME.'

Soon, it was time for plan B. We weren't a team of eleven; we were a squad of twenty-three. We knew that if we stuck together as a group, we still had the depth and quality to fight back and win. **And that's exactly what happened.** In the fifty-eighth minute, **Ellen White** and I came off, and on came two top-class replacements: **Alessia Russo** and **Ella Toone**. Obviously, I didn't want to go off, **but it wasn't about me as an individual**; it was about making the right call for the team. I knew Alessia and Ella could make a difference, and they did! With ten minutes to go, they combined to score the equaliser.

After that, our mindset switched to: 'Right, we do not lose this game'. **Together**, as a squad, we were too strong for Spain, and in extra time, **Georgia Stanway** scored the winner. **We had done it; we had fought back to win and reach the Euro semi-finals!**

IN PRACTICE:

If things are going wrong, always stick together and stay positive. **Encourage the people around you to keep going and fight back.**

If someone makes a mistake, **BE KIND TO THEM,** because moaning and groaning won't do any good!

If you see that one of your teammates is feeling **sad**, go over and talk to them and see if you can help. Either do it at the time or quietly check in with them at the end of the match; whichever feels right in that particular situation and for that particular person. And if you're the one feeling sad, remember that **your teammates will support you – YOU ARE NOT ALONE.**

2) BALANCE FOCUS WITH FUN

Sometimes, when it comes to competitions or tournaments, sport can start to feel **very serious** and **stressful**, but always remember to **ENJOY YOURSELF** too. It's the same with a class presentation at school or a big team project. Because if you're having fun together, you'll be more relaxed and more likely to do your best work.

From the moment Sarina took over as England manager, she took the pressure off and made us all feel much more chilled, both on and off the pitch. That was massive for us. Ahead of the tournament, she didn't say we *were* going to win it. Instead, she said **we wanted to win it**, which was true, but obviously every team wanted to win the Euros! That's pretty unusual in the world of sport. Often, coaches try to make their players believe by telling them, 'You ARE going to win!', but this can sometimes put too much pressure on you, stopping you from performing at your best. Remember, as I said way back at the beginning of this book, **SPORT IS SUPPOSED TO BE FUN**!

Freedom and **fun** can make such a difference to team spirit. I can remember going abroad to an England youth tournament, where we stayed in an amazing, five-star hotel with its own water park, but our coaches said we weren't allowed to use any of the facilities. If we weren't training or playing matches, we were

162

stuck in our hotel rooms all day, with nothing to do. Surprise, surprise, we didn't win the tournament, but the team that did had sunbathed all week and had loads of fun at the water park! They were relaxed and ready to play football, whereas we were **frustrated** and **bored**.

But at the Euros in 2022, we were like that winning team. Sarina trusted us to get the balance right between focus and fun. When we trained, we trained with **100% DEDICATION**, but once the session ended, we chilled. We had time to ourselves, time to switch off, and time to hang out with our families and feel normal. That's where we got it right, compared to tournaments in the past.

At our hotel, the set-up was perfect for keeping us **calm**, **entertained**, and **united**. There was a drinks stand where we could all sit and chat, and a games room with a PlayStation, a dart board and a basketball arcade machine that I got obsessed with. I teamed up with Ellen and we got the top score, but then my wrist started hurting, so I had to stop playing. In fact, I ended up having to wear strapping around my hand for most of the Euro matches, and we think it was probably

from too much basketball! After I retired, **Millie Bright** became Ellen's new basketball partner, and together, they absolutely smashed our score!

We were also right next to the River Thames, so when the weather was nice, we were able to go out on a boat and sunbathe and swim. One night, one of the actors from *The Lion King* came from the Lyceum Theatre in London to sing some songs for us. **WHY? BECAUSE WE'RE THE LIONESSES, DUH!**

With all that entertainment around us, we were able to stay in our own **fun little bubble** throughout the tournament, away from all the media attention. I think that was important, because if we had known what was going on, it would have put so much pressure on us.

It was only on the way to the semi-final against Sweden that we started to realise how many people were following our journey. As our team bus drove through the streets of Sheffield towards the stadium, there were **crowds everywhere, cheering as we passed**.

WOW, THIS WAS BIG, REALLY BIG!

And it was also another semi-final. We had been knocked out in the semi-finals of our last two tournaments, so could we finally break the curse and overcome that obstacle? **YES, WE COULD.** This time, we didn't let the big-game pressure get to us. The first fifteen minutes were pretty cagey, but after that, we settled down and started playing well. **What we needed now was a goal to calm any last nerves . . .**

The move started on the left wing, with **Rachel Daly** passing to **Lauren Hemp**, who whipped the ball into the box. Her cross flew just past Ellen's outstretched boot, and I was inches away from reaching it too. So close! **I didn't switch off, though.** I stayed alert, and when **Lucy Bronze** crossed it back in from the right, I was ready and waiting. My first touch set me up perfectly and I slammed a shot past the keeper to score my sixth goal of the tournament. 1–0 - **WE WERE ON OUR WAY!**

The year before, I might have thought, 'Oh I'm not going to get there, so I'm not going to try,' but I was a different player now, and **we were a different England team**.

After my goal, our shoulders dipped and we relaxed a little. Not too much, but enough to enjoy the semi-final. Lucy headed in from my corner-kick just after half-time, and then Alessia made it 3–0 with a bit of skill that summed up **our confidence and fun-loving spirit**. Her first shot was saved, but as the ball rebounded out to her, she fired a cheeky back-heel through the keeper's legs and into the net!

Fran Kirby's fourth goal was pretty cheeky too, a chip over the keeper's head from outside the box. **WOW**, we were flying, and we were **on our way through to the Euro final!**

Once the match was over, we allowed ourselves time to celebrate together. Yes, we still had one more game to win, but we wanted to enjoy every moment along the way. So in the photographs, some of us are wearing scarves, Rachel's wearing a cowboy hat, and all of us are smiling and roaring at the camera. **We look more like people at a fancy dress party than a football team!**

The next day, we were fully focused again, and we worked harder than ever in the days leading up to the final. But even in the dressing room at Wembley, before the biggest game of all our lives, Sarina's message was exactly the same:

'It's just another game of football – go out there and enjoy it. We don't have to win it, but we really want to win it.'

GET READY TO ROAR ACTIVITY

What could you do to make sure your team is having fun together?

Maybe you could suggest a fun activity for everyone to do during the warm-up at training, or maybe you could organise a team camping trip or sleepover. But please, check with the grown-ups at home first, **OK?** And don't forget the marshmallows!

Whatever you choose to do, it's always a good idea to get a nice **balance between hard work and fun**. Too much fun, and we can lose our focus. Too much hard work, and we can lose interest and motivation.

And that doesn't only apply to sport; it applies to **anything in life**. If you're revising for a test, for example, you shouldn't just sit and study all the time. It's important to also go out for walks and get plenty of fresh air and, of course, spend time having fun with your friends.

3) WORK TOGETHER, WIN TOGETHER

THERE'S NO 'I' IN 'TEAM'

– that's another phrase that you've probably heard before, but it's important. No matter how good you are or how big your role, no single member is more important than the team. **You work together, you win together** – it's as simple as that.

There were twenty-three members of our England Euro squad and we all played our part. We all worked so hard, and not for our own personal glory, but for each other. For the team. **THAT WAS KEY TO OUR SUCCESS.**

Whenever Sarina subbed a player off, her decision was accepted without any arguments because it was in the **best interests of the team**. If the starting XI weren't winning the match, then we trusted the great players on the bench to come on and change the game. Alessia and Ella had done it in the quarter-finals against Spain, and in the final against Germany, it was Ella and Chloe Kelly's turn.

But before we get on to all that, let me go back to the **beginning** of that amazing night. As much as we tried to treat it like 'just another game of football', we knew that it was massive. We were in a major international final in front of our home fans; it doesn't get much bigger than that. As we walked out at Wembley to the sound of eighty-seven thousand supporters and looked up to see the proud faces of our families, it was an **incredibly emotional moment**.

We didn't let that affect our focus, though. **No**, we had a match to win and a trophy to lift, and through working together, we were determined to get the job done, no matter what.

The first half was a very physical and even battle. Both teams had a few good chances to score, but it stayed 0–0, so early in the second half, Sarina began to switch things up, with Ella and Alessia coming on for Fran and Ellen.

What about me – would I get to stay on for the full game? I was hoping so, but in the sixtieth minute, I went in for a big tackle and ended up with a really painful dead leg. When I got back up, I could hardly walk, let alone run. **UH OH, WHAT WAS I GOING TO DO?**

Obviously, I desperately wanted to stay out on the pitch and play on. The Euros had been the best tournament of my life and I wanted to end it in style with a golden moment in the final. But it wasn't just about me; my decision would affect all of the Lionesses. **I KNEW WHAT WAS BEST FOR THE SAKE OF MY TEAM.**

'I've given everything I've got,' I thought to myself. 'I need to let someone come on who can do a better job than I can in these last thirty minutes.'

Missing a massive moment is always disappointing, but sometimes you've got to look at the **bigger picture**. If you're injured or unwell, there might be someone else in a better position to get the job done. It's about **shifting your perspective** from what's best for you to **what's best for everyone**. **THAT'S WHAT IT MEANS TO BE A REAL TEAM PLAYER.**

While I limped off and Chloe got ready to replace me, England had only ten players on the pitch, but that didn't make us weaker. **If anything, it made us stronger. Keira Walsh** got the ball in midfield and played a beautiful long pass through to Ella, who kept calm and chipped the keeper. 1–0!

For the next few moments, it was as if my injury had magically disappeared. I turned to the fans, screaming and jumping for joy.

WE WERE WINNING
IN THE EURO FINAL!

As soon as I stopped celebrating, however, the pain returned. 'Owww, I shouldn't have done that!' I told myself. Oh well, I would just have to watch the rest of the match from the sidelines.

The next hour turned out to be **the most stressful hour of my life**! After going 1–0 up, we did what a lot of teams do in that position: we sat too deep in defence and invited Germany forward on the attack, until eventually **they scored an equaliser**.

In the end, the game went all the way to extra time, but my teammates never gave up or stopped believing in each other. Everyone played their part, from the starters to the subs. **Jill Scott** and **Alex Greenwood** came on and brought calm and experience to the team, and Chloe, my replacement? **Well, she scored the winner, didn't she!**

When the goal went in, my injury magically disappeared again. I hurdled the barriers and raced on to the pitch with the rest of the subs. **Surely we had won the Euro final now?** There were still ten more anxious minutes to go, but the Lionesses kept hold of the ball brilliantly until at last **the final whistle blew.**

WE HAD DONE IT – WE HAD WORKED TOGETHER AND WON TOGETHER.

WE WERE THE CHAMPIONS OF EUROPE!

Later on, as we stood there celebrating on the pitch, I was presented with two extra trophies of my own: **TOP SCORER** and **BEST PLAYER**. Of course, I was delighted to win the awards, but in that moment, all I wanted to do was dance with the other Lionesses, my friends. **That was the most important thing for me.** I cared more about being a part of the group than any individual award because **I WOULDN'T HAVE WON ANYTHING WITHOUT MY TEAMMATES**.

So whether you're playing sport, performing a play or putting on a school assembly, remember that **teamwork makes the dream work**. When you support each other, have fun together, work together and win together, amazing things can happen. If you didn't believe it before, I hope you do now because just look what we Lionesses achieved!

Heroes: THE LIONESSES

I want to say a big thank you to every member of the England camp. I'll start with my twenty-two teammates, the best group of friends I could ever have asked for:

1 Mary Earps	10 Georgia Stanway
2 Lucy Bronze	11 Lauren Hemp
3 Rachel Daly	12 Jess Carter
4 Keira Walsh	13 Hannah Hampton
5 Alex Greenwood	14 Fran Kirby
6 Millie Bright	15 Demi Stokes
7 Me!	16 Jill Scott
8 Leah Williamson	17 Nikita Parris
9 Ellen White	18 Chloe Kelly

19 Bethany England

20 Ella Toone

21 Ellie Roebuck

22 Lotte Wubben-Moy

23 Alessia Russo

Next, I want to thank **Sarina** and all the **coaches**, **physios** and staff who helped prepare us so well to go out there and win. As I said before, **BEHIND EVERY SUCCESS IS A BIG TEAM EFFORT**.

And finally, I want to thank **all the incredible fans**, who cheer us all the way to victory. **YOU'RE ALL HEROES AND WE COULDN'T DO WHAT WE DO WITHOUT YOU!!**

BETH'S TOP THREE GREATEST TROPHIES:

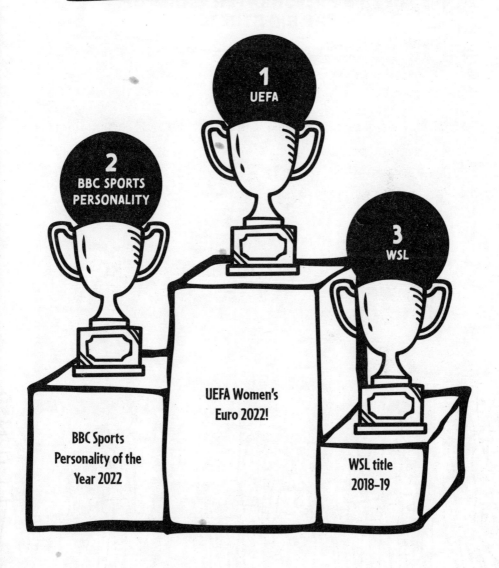

2 BBC SPORTS PERSONALITY

1 UEFA

3 WSL

BBC Sports Personality of the Year 2022

UEFA Women's Euro 2022!

WSL title 2018–19

BETH'S PRE-CHAPTER WARM-UP: THE BIG STRETCH

Everyone talks about warming up, but it's good to warm down too, once your hard work is over. So, seeing as this is the final chapter, let's have one last S-T-R-E-T-C-H together. It's good for:

- ✓ Relieving achy and tight muscles
- ✓ Warming up/waking up the body
- ✓ Helping posture and balance

WHAT TO DO: From a standing position, bend over at the waist and try to reach down and touch your toes with your fingers. If you can't quite reach your toes, don't worry! Just stretch as far as it feels comfortable and then stop.

EXTRA TIME: For more of a challenge, try crossing your legs over as you stand, and then reach down and touch your toes.

CHAPTER ELEVEN

ENJOY EVERY MOMENT

As we lifted the Euro trophy at Wembley in front of eighty-seven thousand fans, it was without doubt the **GREATEST ACHIEVEMENT OF MY CAREER** so far. We had made history, becoming not only the first England football team to win a major international tournament since 1966, but also the first England football team - men's or women's - to **EVER** win the Euros! It was a huge moment for us as players, but it was also a huge moment for the women's game in general. Finally people were paying attention and showing us the respect that our performances deserved. That night at Wembley, as the Euros came to an end, it felt like the start of something very special. Women's football was on the rise, reaching a whole new audience and a whole new level, and we Lionesses were very proud to play our part.

When you achieve something amazing, after lots of hard work and dedication, you've got to make the most of it.

Appreciate what you've done.

Take it all in.

Savour the full experience.

Soak up the atmosphere.

Feel every emotion.

Enjoy every moment.

Because you deserve it!

I found my best football form by going back to the beginning and playing like a little kid again, having fun and feeling free. So I want this book to end by going back to the beginning too.

Do you remember what I called the very first chapter of this book? (No, don't cheat by flicking back through the pages!)

The answer is . . . **JUMP IN AND ENJOY!** (Well done, if you got it right!)

So it felt right to call this, the very last chapter . . . **ENJOY EVERY MOMENT**.

I think sport is amazing for lots of different reasons that I've talked about throughout this book: **the friendships, the dreams, the teamwork, the resilience, the fitness, the focus** – but the best and most important reason of all is . . . the **FUN**! Because if you're not having fun, what's the point in playing?

As you **chase your dreams**, there will be lots of ups and downs, high and lows. That's how it was for me, anyway, and so you've got to ride the lows when they come, and then really, really enjoy the highs. Even the little wins in life are important and worth celebrating.

This applies to all your successes. Sometimes when we do well, we can often think: 'OK, what next?' without celebrating what we've achieved already! Earlier on in my football career, there were times when I achieved great things – goals, trophies, playing in a World Cup – but I let them pass me by. I didn't sit and reflect enough on them until it was a bit too late to live those moments, but not any more.

That night when we won the Euro final, I made sure that **I took it all in and enjoyed every moment of it. THE SONGS, THE DANCES, THE PHOTOS, THE HUGS, THE LAUGHS, THE TEARS . . . ALL OF IT.** As I ran around the pitch with my England teammates, I had so many different emotions running through my body: **relief, excitement, shock, pride** . . . There was a lot going on, but when you're enjoying the moment, you remember it more.

Once we'd finished celebrating on the pitch, we carried the party on in the changing room and then into Sarina's post-match press conference too. As she sat there talking to the journalists, we burst in through the door, and then bounced up and down with our gold medals around our necks, singing **'FOOTBALL'S COMING HOME!'** at the top of our voices. **Lucy Bronze** and **Mary Earps** even got up and started dancing on the tables!

The next few days were a blur, a happy blur, the best kind of blur possible. After a couple of hours' sleep with my **medal around my neck**, I was awake again, having some much-needed breakfast before we made our way to Trafalgar Square for the England Champions Party.

AND WHAT A PARTY IT WAS! As our bus arrived, the streets were already filled with cheering fans and waving flags. **It all felt like a dream.** Was this actually happening? What had we done? Had we really just won the Euros? Yes, we had!

When we eventually got to the stage, I looked out at what seemed like a never-ending sea of people. Seven thousand people, who were all there to see us and celebrate with us. **Unbelievable!** There was lots more singing and some speeches too. I wasn't expecting to have to talk, but suddenly, I heard my name and my teammates were pulling me to the front.

Oh no, what was I going to say? How could I possibly put my emotions into words? It wasn't easy, but I managed to say something:

'I feel so lucky to be part of this team and be a part of this group. I'm just so happy to be here. I'm so happy.'

I was enjoying every moment. When the Champions Party finished, we still weren't ready to say goodbye and stop celebrating. We wanted to keep the winning feeling going for as long as we could. So we all went back to our homes, got changed and then met up again to go out as a team in London. I'm so glad we had that extra night to have fun together and also to look back at what we had achieved.

GET READY TO ROAR ACTIVITY

Next time you achieve something brilliant, I want you to remember to take a pause and really celebrate what you've done. **Congratulate yourself on how far you've come. Be proud of yourself. Enjoy the moment.** And remember, whether it's a smaller win or a bigger win, it's still a win, and it's still worth celebrating!

Speaking of celebrating, I hope you've got your victory dance ready! **If not, why not?** Now's the time to come up with your own fun, unique way to enjoy every success. A conga around the classroom? Knee-slides across the sports pitch? The robot around your bedroom? It's up to YOU (and your teammates)!

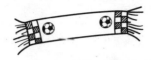

Winning all the big tournaments has always been our main goal, but the Lionesses also want to have a **wider impact on women's sport, in England and all around the world**. We want to show what we can do to take the game to the next level: with more exciting performances, more excited people are watching the game.

In the past, the women's game has often been thought of as second to the men's game. **But that's all changing**.

Our ambition is for **BIGGER WINS, MORE SUCCESSES** and inspiring **more people to watch us play**.

We also want to inspire the next generation – **that's you!** – to dream big and follow their sporting passions. That's why the Lionesses signed a letter to the government, asking for a **minimum of two hours of PE per week for girls as well as boys**. Everyone deserves to enjoy playing football in the playground and during PE lessons at school.

HERO: YOU, THE READER!

First of all, I want to say a big thank you for reading my book – it means so much to me. I hope you've enjoyed my story and that it has also inspired you to find a sport you love, work hard at everything you do and achieve your dreams. So what are you waiting for?

JUMP IN AND ENJOY the world of sport,

BE HAPPY IN WHO YOU ARE AND CREATE YOUR OWN KIND OF FUN,

DREAM BIG AND SET YOUR SUPERSTAR GOALS,

BUT DON'T STAY IN THE SHALLOW END (FOR EVER),

TAKE THINGS ONE STEP AT A TIME,

GET INSPIRED AND RAISE YOUR GAME,

LET DISAPPOINTMENTS DRIVE YOU ON,

FLICK THAT SUPERSTAR SWITCH,

BELIEVE IN YOURSELF (LIKE OTHERS BELIEVE IN YOU),

WORK TOGETHER, WIN TOGETHER

and ENJOY EVERY MOMENT

Got all that? Good, you've got this. You're ready.

NOW LET ME HEAR YOU ROAR!!!!!!!

BETH'S TOP THREE GREATEST MOMENTS:

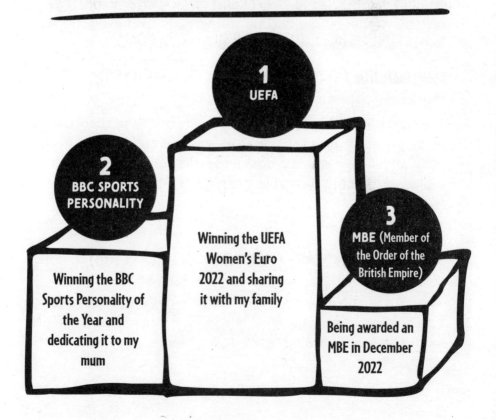

2 BBC SPORTS PERSONALITY

Winning the BBC Sports Personality of the Year and dedicating it to my mum

1 UEFA

Winning the UEFA Women's Euro 2022 and sharing it with my family

3 MBE (Member of the Order of the British Empire)

Being awarded an MBE in December 2022

RESOURCES

McDonald's Fun Football Centres
www.mcdonalds.com/gb/en-gb/football/fun-football-centres.html

I think it's so important to make getting into sport as easy as possible, and that's why I'm working with McDonald's on their Fun Football Centres project, which provides free coaching sessions for kids aged five to eleven across England. The sessions are a fun introduction to the game and everyone is welcome, no matter what their football ability!

Youth Sport Trust
www.youthsporttrust.org

The Youth Sport Trust aims to give every child the chance to enjoy the life-changing benefits of play and sport. Through a range of different sports programmes, they give young people a platform to have their voice heard and a place to feel they belong.

Weetabix Wildcats
www.weetabix.co.uk/weetabix-wildcats

Weetabix Wildcats is non-competitive football for girls who want to give it a go for the very first time or want to play with other girls their own age. Most importantly, it's all about having loads of fun and meeting new amazing friends.

England Football
www.englandfootball.com

This is the place to go to find out more about your England heroes, and it's also the place to go to find a football team or session near you. So go on, get involved!

Premier League Primary Stars
www.plprimarystars.com

Premier League Primary Stars uses the appeal of the Premier League and professional football clubs to inspire children to be active and develop important literacy and life skills, like resilience and self-esteem.

Chance to Shine
www.chancetoshine.org

If cricket is, or could be, your sport, then check out Chance to Shine. It's a national charity that aims to give all children the opportunity to play, learn and develop through cricket. Chance to Shine offer coaching sessions in schools and also in local communities.

funetics
www.funetics.co.uk

Or maybe you like athletics, like me? funetics is a fun and inclusive kids athletics programme, created by England Athletics to help four- to eleven-year-old children across the country to learn, develop and practise running, jumping and throwing skills all year round, for a healthy confident future.

Goalball UK
www.goalballuk.com

Goalball is an accessible three-a-side team sport for people who are blind or partially sighted, which involves bowling the ball along the floor and into the other team's net. Goalball UK is an inclusive organisation which gives people opportunities to participate and compete at all levels.

Activity Alliance
www.activityalliance.org.uk

Activity Alliance believe in creating a fairer world where everyone can be active however and wherever they want to be, by making sport more inclusive for disabled people.

NHS: Accessible activities
www.nhs.uk/healthier-families/activities/accessible-activities

The NHS offers lots of ideas for fun games and activities to help disabled children stay active – at home, with the rest of the family or through a National Disability Sports Organisation. Why not take a look with your parent or carer?

Scope
www.scope.org.uk/advice-and-support/disability-sport/#Finding-accessible-sports-click

Scope is a charity that works to make the world fairer and equal for disabled people, and they have a great list of ideas for finding and taking part in accessible sports.